Chang

Hypnosis

Relaxing Guided Meditations for Weight Loss, Alcohol and Food Addiction - Stop Smoking, Eliminate Bad Habits & Feel Healthier + 342 Powerful Self Affirmations

Written By

342 Powerful Self Affirmations

Contents

Disclaimer

Do not listen to this audiobook while driving or operating heavy machinery.

While hypnosis, hypnotherapy and energy work may have beneficial and positive effects, it is not a substitute for appropriate medical attention. Guided meditations and self hypnosis tracks inside this audiobook are not a substitute or a replacement for the practice of psychology or psychiatry.

Nor are they intended to treat, cure or diagnose any disease, condition or illness. When dealing with a physical and/or mental illness, always consult a qualified physician or therapist.

Hypnotherapy downloads are not recommended for persons experiencing mental disorders or illness.

Never disregard professional medical advice, or delay in seeking it, because of something you have heard or interpreted within this audiobook.

Never rely on information within this audiobook, or on the internet, in place of seeking professional medical advice. Persons with an ailment or physical complaint are to see their physician first for treatment, and make use of hypnosis and hypnotherapy as an adjunct to medical treatment. Persons with mental disabilities or mental illnesses should seek psychiatric care.

Overcoming Addiction - A Visual Short Story

Do not listen to this audio recording while driving or operating heavy machinery. Thank you.

Welcome to this guided meditation for allowing the law of attraction to bring abundance, wealth, success, love and miracles into your life.

Now, if you haven't used a guided meditation or hypnosis tape before, it's important to know that you understand what is happening to your body throughout this recording.

When you are in the state of self-hypnosis, you are not asleep, nor are you unconscious.

You're actually very aware of your surroundings, and you can't be coerced into doing anything which you don't want to.

So don't worry about any external distractions or noises because you will soon be able to relax completely.

You are always in complete control of yourself.

I will be saying a series of prompts, you can hear the suggestions and prompts as you wish.

Just allow yourself to absorb the suggestions without thinking or trying to analyze them.

And don't worry if your mind drifts off somewhere else.

You will still gain a positive outcome from the prompts and if you find yourself focusing on other thoughts, you can slowly remind yourself to focus only on my voice and what I am saying.

And don't worry if you don't think you are "getting it" or doing it right. Especially if this is your first time. There is no right or wrong way to go about this.

Just allow yourself to feel comfortable and relaxed.

Start in a comfortable position, either sitting or laying down.

And now, begin by taking just a few deep breaths, in through your nose and out through your mouth.

Really focus your attention where you feel the breath.

For some of you, that will be your nose, for some it will be your chest, and for others, you will feel it in your belly.

Wherever that place is for you, just bring your attention to that part of your body, and breathe.

If it helps, you can count the breaths as they go.

pause for 20 seconds

If you feel your mind wandering, then just bring your attention back to the breath, and feel it coming in through the nose and out through the mouth.

And as you go into a deeper state of relaxation, you will become more receptive to the words you are hearing.

Now, as you exhale this time, I want you to visualize a tree root going through you, and anchoring itself to the earth below you.

This root is your grounding root, it helps you stay centered throughout the meditation, and will provide comfort and warmth during your experience.

It also helps you focus if you mind becomes distracted.

But for now, just really feel the root anchoring itself to the ground beneath you, and how sturdy and firm you feel in your body.

You're doing great, just allow your body to expand and keep breathing in through your nose and out through your mouth.

By allowing this cord to anchor, you can release nay negative tension by sending it along the cord, so it disperses out into the earth around you.

By doing this, the tension moves out of your body, and into the world around you.

You can release any stress, tension or anxiety at any time during this meditation by releasing it along the root, and out into the universe.

Take another deep breath.

You are becoming aware of just how relaxed you are during the process.

Of how in control of your destiny you truly are

You are in the best place you could be right now.

You are in the best place you could be right now.

You are in the best place you could be right now.

Take another deep breath.

I want you to begin consciously focusing on relaxing your muscles.

We'll start at the top of your head.

Begin to feel a soothing wave of relaxation flowing down through the very top of your head.

Feel this wave caress over the crown of your head, and around the side of your head until it touches your ears.

Feel it slowly tricking down over your eyebrows, as each bit of relaxation touches your skin.

Allow it to move around the side of your eyes, as feel your face getting slightly heavier with each moment that passes.

You are at ease and you feel completely comfortable right now.

Just allow your ears to focus in on the sound of my voice, and feel the relaxation continue to move down your body.

Your muscles may even feel like they're melting slightly, this is a good thing.

And just like ice melts under the warm sun, your muscles are melting down with this wave of relaxation.

Allow this wave to come past your jaw and down into your neck.

Through your tongue and your teeth.

If you feel slightly tingly at this point, don't worry, that's completely normal – you are relaxing your muscles and going deeper into your subconscious mind

Allow the wave of relaxation to flow down the back and front of your beck, and from your head into your upper torso and upper back.

With every breathe you take you are drifting deeper and deeper into a relaxed state.

Across your shoulders and then down into your chest and back.

You are solely focused on your body right now.

Expand your chest and back as you continue to breathe.

Allowing the wave of relaxation to reach every inch of your body.

Really feel the relaxation in your muscles and tendons of your body.

And allow this relaxation to melt your muscles just like ice on a warm summer's day.

Feel the comforting warmth of relaxation across your body.

And let it keep moving down across your body down into your elbows and arms.

And further down into your fingertips.

You might feel some tingling in your fingers, don't worry, this is completely normal.

Just let this relaxation move all over your body.

Let it spread down through your belly and into your hips.

This will open you up and allow your subconscious to receive the prompts.

Now it is just you, and my voice guiding you.

As you sink deeper and deeper into a relaxed state of mind.

Allow the wave to go down into your thighs, and then down into your lower legs.

Slowly orbiting your ankles with comfort and ease.

This wave moves down deeper and deeper as we move further.

Across your calves as it relaxes your lower leg muscles, you are truly relaxed now.

Allow it to move down through your ankles, and finally into your feet.

Watch it move across the soles of your feet, as well as the tops of them.

And finally, down into your toes.

Feel the tingling of your toes as the relaxation flows through you.

Now, you are truly primed and ready to be guided on a journey to greatness.

You can imagine your root grounding you as well.

In this position, only positive effects can occur in the next 45 minutes.

Because you have allowed yourself to relax, open up, and embrace the positive changes you are about to have come into your life.

Anything is possible for you at this point.

Anything and everything is possible.

You can overcome even your biggest challenge, no matter how insurmountable that might seem right now.

In just a few seconds, I will begin to count down from five. After this, you will transported into a new world.

A world where anything is possible, and you can make the changes you want to make in life.

And as I count down, with each number, your level of relaxation will instantly increase.

Don't fight this, don't force it, just let it happen. Here we go.

Five, keep breathing, and feel yourself sinking deeper and deeper down.

Four, you are so relaxed now.

Three, just existing and letting go. It feels so good to just let go.

Two. Getting even closer now, now, peacefully, comfortably relaxed,

And one.

Take a deep breath in through the nose, out through the mouth.

Imagine yourself standing on a white sand beach overlooking the ocean, the water a beautiful blue and the sun coming up in the early morning of the day ahead. It's a beautiful summer's day and the warm sun comes up for an enjoyable feeling all around. The breeze from the water comes and touches your skin softly, and you like the sensation.

There is not even a single cloud in the blue sky.

Looking up, you see the sun and it hits you with peace. You enjoy the colors of the sun.

You smell the salty water, the sense touching your nose softly and waking you up as you listen to the sounds of the waves gently reaching the beach and breaking a few feet in front of you. The air is cool, a perfect temperature for your liking, not too hot, and not too cold. You enjoy this feeling, it makes you joyful and happy. As the sun's rays touch your skin, you rejoice at the sensation of them reaching your face and hands.

This way, you begin to sink into an ideal state of relaxation, as you follow the rhythm of the breath.

You are doing great this way.

The moment you gaze at the waters of the vast ocean in front of you, you are a step closer to calmness, relaxation and a step further from stress.

Sit with the feeling for a moment and see the stress being taken away by the ocean.

The sun continues to rise and enhance the scenery in front of you.

With each meter the sun grows taller in the sky, you are sinking deeper and deeper into calmness, bliss and joyfulness. The tension of the body dissipates with each second passing.

Your entire negativity is now ready to depart forever from your being.

You are finally ready to leave all worries behind you. This is your time to feel at peace with the body and the mind. Whatever has happened in the past, it is now ready to be left behind.

Follow the flow of your breathing, continue like this while admiring the perfect water and the soft moves of the winds coming back and forward towards you.

Sit with the feeling for 1 minute

In your mind, begin walking with your feet on the beach, as you look at the vastity of the ocean. There are no more worries for you.

As you walk along the sand, you notice that your breath is becoming softer and deeper, as your body gets overflowing with relaxation. Stress is getting out of your system, the negative part of your being is getting out of you. Visualise these thoughts and emotions from above.

This happens as the sun keeps reflecting its rays in the ocean's water.

The water is calm, the waves are barely reaching a feet.

The calmness and relaxing atmosphere is perfect.

As you move along, you see a beach chair somewhere on the sand.

Getting closer to the chair, you feel the need to sit in it.

Once in the chair, you realise that it is very comfortable.

The chair you're sitting on is made out of the perfect materials, has the ideal height and makes you feel great while in it.

You are filled with calmness while you're in the chair.

The mind sends you thoughts of peace, joy, happiness, bliss.

Now, the mind takes you someplace else, some place where everything you want is a possibility.

This can be a new place or a place where you've been to before.

See yourself in the place right now, the first one that comes to mind.

The conscious part of the mind gets you to this place now. The part of the mind that's focusing on practice is the one in power, letting you decide the intensity and the reality of the things you're thinking about and acting upon.

Visualise the place that comes to mind at first.

This place is important because it has a strong connection with safety.

The place is rooted within, coming with very good reasons for you to feel calm and safe, to be deeply rooted into the senses and the elements, bringing a sense of peace and acceptance of who you are in your deepest self.

Focus on this feeling for a moment and appreciate it.

No harm can be casted upon you while here. Visualise the motives why this place is so calm and safe for you.

Now, imagine a beam of light coming down upon you, a protector made out of yellow light, big and bright enough so that you can move inside it.

You can still see the ocean outside, still hear the waves and still feel the breeze, yet there is no negativity that can come inside the safe beam of light.

Please, touch the walls of the beam of light for a moment.

Describe the beam in your mind right now. How bright is it? How does it feel?

This beam of light works as a source for all things, mainly for positivity and removing negativity out of your life.

You are in control while you're in the beam.

The beam is now a part of you. Every time you think about the light, you are getting more and more relaxed, happy and worry-free.

The more you practice, the better these feelings will get integrated in the mind.

The beam of light, just by bringing it up, will make you feel stronger every day.

Stress and all the tensions will begin to melt, you will be in complete control of your mind and body, of thoughts and emotions.

Wherever you are, whatever you do, this is your safe place from now on.

The moment you mentally step inside it, you are protected from all negativity.

Remember to practice the power of the beam of light each day, remembering its benefits and relieving the feelings of peace, power and tranquility it provided during this meditation practice.

The more you practice the feelings, the stronger they'll become in the mind.

Your end goal is to become a better, stronger, permanently calmer version of your own self, with a mind that's powerful over negativity and stress.

Get ready to make a few changes in your life, now that you have all of this new energy and positivity standing by your side.

Now it's the time to speak to the person inside you.

The deepest you, tell him about your unfortunate habits.

Tell the deepest version of you about your addictions and why you're ready to remove them.

Tell the mind that controls your emotions and habits you're ready to get over your addictions.

Tell the mind you're in control now, you can command the ship of your own being entirely.

The highest level of control is your own now, you are powerful enough so that you can decide your own fate regarding addiction.

You know that putting alcohol or drugs into your system is bad, and that addiction starts the moment you do this simple action, in your own mind. Remember that addiction starts in the mind and ends in the mind.

Addiction starts in the mind at first. Ask your true self about it, and you'll notice everything happens in the mind at first.

After this practice ends today, you'll begin to develop a new set of habits that will make you free from addiction.

You are now building the foundation of a better version of yourself.

In the mind, you find this foundation of the new you awesome.

This new you is blissful and happy and beautiful without any external help.

This new you is conscious about health and keeping himself away from bad habits. This new you is addiction-free.

This new you leaves addictions aside because he's no longer in need for any external sources of happiness.

This new you feels better without drugs or alcohol.

Enter this cycle of joy, both internal and external.

The more joyful you are, the less the urge for addiction.

The less the urge for addiction, the more joyful you are.

The calmer you are, the less you need to become addicted.

The less you need to become addicted, the calmer you are.

The more peaceful you are, the less addictive you are.

The less addictive you are, the more peaceful you are.

The less you give into addiction, the happier you are.

The happier you are, the less addictive you become.

You are becoming stronger, better, healthier every time you remind yourself of this cycle of self-inflicted happiness and joy.

Your entire being wants to become stronger, healthier and better and that being is deeply rooted within you.

You have a choice to be this better version of your own self every moment of every day.

Feel good about this opportunity and chose wisely.

No matter what might happen in life, you can always experience this new, better version of your own self, this healthier version, this addiction-free version of you just by doing the practice as needed while you live your life.

There is no more addiction inside you, which allows you to restore your health.

The body and the mind are capable of taking care of themselves in a natural way, with no danger from drugs or alcohol.

With each day you're staying away from addictive habits, you get better at it.

With each day it gets easier and more manageable to be positive and healthy.

Your life is so much more interesting and exciting without addiction, you are in complete control of the mind and body, naturally enhancing the experience of life and all you feel and sense around you.

Take the time to appreciate this new you and the body you're accustomed to.

Develop a new sense of calm and clarity, which will help you to realise how much of a mistake addiction was for you.

Be present in the now, in this very moment, without the usage of drugs or other substances.

Exercise being present in the moment every single day, as you will get better at it every single day.

This practice will keep you healthy and anchored in the present.

See yourself in the mind in five years from now, addiction-free.

See yourself as a mature, healthy, powerful individual, how would that make you feel, what is your posture.

Go a step further and imagine yourself surrounded by a happy wife, kids and family, all around the dinner table enjoying food and company.

Imagine the joy you'll feel when the people you love will be there for you for longer.

Get ready for a change, take a deep breath and enjoy life more starting from now.

Feel the new energies around you, energies you've never experienced before, coming down your body and mind just as it happened a second ago with the beam of light on the beach.

The new energy comes and touches the mind and the body.

The new energy is from within and is healthy for your entire being.

The new energy makes you healthy and addiction-free. You haven't had a glass of alcohol in a while, and you don't need one.

All that you've achieved is by yourself, all because you've decided to leave the habit of addiction in the past.

Addiction-free, your are now happier than ever.

This new path you're on is a positive one, a new, exciting one.

Focus on this feeling and be grateful for it.

Sit with this feeling for a minute

You are now ready to come back to the material world.

Wiggle your fingers and toes now.

Remove yourself from the depths of the mind and come back.

Start noticing the body from the top of the head at first.

Move down the back, chest and stomach and middle of the body.

Go all the way down to the feet and toes.

Start a short count from five to one, as you begin to regroup into the material world around you.

Five. Begin your journey back to the conscious mind.

Four. Notice the weight of your body.

Three. Sense the smells, sounds and feelings from your surroundings.

Two. Take on final, deep breath in through the nose, out through the mouth.

One. Open your eyes, relax and take a moment to feel great about this moment.

Stop Smoking - A Visual Short Story

Do not listen to this audio recording while driving or operating heavy machinery. Thank you.

Welcome to this guided meditation for allowing the law of attraction to bring abundance, wealth, success, love and miracles into your life.

Now, if you haven't used a guided meditation or hypnosis tape before, it's important to know that you understand what is happening to your body throughout this recording.

When you are in the state of self-hypnosis, you are not asleep, nor are you unconscious.

You're actually very aware of your surroundings, and you can't be coerced into doing anything which you don't want to.

So don't worry about any external distractions or noises because you will soon be able to relax completely.

You are always in complete control of yourself.

I will be saying a series of prompts, you can hear the suggestions and prompts as you wish.

Just allow yourself to absorb the suggestions without thinking or trying to analyze them.

And don't worry if your mind drifts off somewhere else.

You will still gain a positive outcome from the prompts and if you find yourself focusing on other thoughts, you can slowly remind yourself to focus only on my voice and what I am saying.

And don't worry if you don't think you are "getting it" or doing it right. Especially if this is your first time. There is no right or wrong way to go about this.

Just allow yourself to feel comfortable and relaxed.

Start in a comfortable position, either sitting or laying down.

And now, begin by taking just a few deep breaths, in through your nose and out through your mouth.

Really focus your attention where you feel the breath.

For some of you, that will be your nose, for some it will be your chest, and for others, you will feel it in your belly.

Wherever that place is for you, just bring your attention to that part of your body, and breathe.

If it helps, you can count the breaths as they go.

pause for 20 seconds

If you feel your mind wandering, then just bring your attention back to the breath, and feel it coming in through the nose and out through the mouth.

And as you go into a deeper state of relaxation, you will become more receptive to the words you are hearing.

Now, as you exhale this time, I want you to visualize a tree root going through you, and anchoring itself to the earth below you.

This root is your grounding root, it helps you stay centered throughout the meditation, and will provide comfort and warmth during your experience.

It also helps you focus if you mind becomes distracted.

But for now, just really feel the root anchoring itself to the ground beneath you, and how sturdy and firm you feel in your body.

You're doing great, just allow your body to expand and keep breathing in through your nose and out through your mouth.

By allowing this cord to anchor, you can release nay negative tension by sending it along the cord, so it disperses out into the earth around you.

By doing this, the tension moves out of your body, and into the world around you.

You can release any stress, tension or anxiety at any time during this meditation by releasing it along the root, and out into the universe.

Take another deep breath.

You are becoming aware of just how relaxed you are during the process.

Of how in control of your destiny you truly are

You are in the best place you could be right now.

You are in the best place you could be right now.

You are in the best place you could be right now.

Take another deep breath.

I want you to begin consciously focusing on relaxing your muscles.

We'll start at the top of your head.

Begin to feel a soothing wave of relaxation flowing down through the very top of your head.

Feel this wave caress over the crown of your head, and around the side of your head until it touches your ears.

Feel it slowly tricking down over your eyebrows, as each bit of relaxation touches your skin.

Allow it to move around the side of your eyes, as feel your face getting slightly heavier with each moment that passes.

You are at ease and you feel completely comfortable right now.

Just allow your ears to focus in on the sound of my voice, and feel the relaxation continue to move down your body.

Your muscles may even feel like they're melting slightly, this is a good thing.

And just like ice melts under the warm sun, your muscles are melting down with this wave of relaxation.

Allow this wave to come past your jaw and down into your neck.

Through your tongue and your teeth.

If you feel slightly tingly at this point, don't worry, that's completely normal – you are relaxing your muscles and going deeper into your subconscious mind

Allow the wave of relaxation to flow down the back and front of your beck, and from your head into your upper torso and upper back.

With every breathe you take you are drifting deeper and deeper into a relaxed state.

Across your shoulders and then down into your chest and back.

You are solely focused on your body right now.

Expand your chest and back as you continue to breathe.

Allowing the wave of relaxation to reach every inch of your body.

Really feel the relaxation in your muscles and tendons of your body.

And allow this relaxation to melt your muscles just like ice on a warm summer's day.

Feel the comforting warmth of relaxation across your body.

And let it keep moving down across your body down into your elbows and arms.

And further down into your fingertips.

You might feel some tingling in your fingers, don't worry, this is completely normal.

Just let this relaxation move all over your body.

Let it spread down through your belly and into your hips.

This will open you up and allow your subconscious to receive the prompts.

Now it is just you, and my voice guiding you.

As you sink deeper and deeper into a relaxed state of mind.

Allow the wave to go down into your thighs, and then down into your lower legs.

Slowly orbiting your ankles with comfort and ease.

This wave moves down deeper and deeper as we move further.

Across your calves as it relaxes your lower leg muscles, you are truly relaxed now.

Allow it to move down through your ankles, and finally into your feet.

Watch it move across the soles of your feet, as well as the tops of them.

And finally, down into your toes.

Feel the tingling of your toes as the relaxation flows through you.

Now, you are truly primed and ready to be guided on a journey to greatness.

You can imagine your root grounding you as well.

In this position, only positive effects can occur in the next 45 minutes.

Because you have allowed yourself to relax, open up, and embrace the positive changes you are about to have come into your life.

Anything is possible for you at this point.

Anything and everything is possible.

You can overcome even your biggest challenge, no matter how insurmountable that might seem right now.

In just a few seconds, I will begin to count down from five. After this, you will transported into a new world.

A world where anything is possible, and you can make the changes you want to make in life.

And as I count down, with each number, your level of relaxation will instantly increase.

Don't fight this, don't force it, just let it happen. Here we go.

Five, keep breathing, and feel yourself sinking deeper and deeper down.

Four, you are so relaxed now.

Three, just existing and letting go. It feels so good to just let go.

Two. Getting even closer now, now, peacefully, comfortably relaxed,

And one.

You find yourself standing on the top of a hill overlooking a beautiful lake in the early morning on a beautiful summer's day. The day starts up warm enough for it to be enjoyable. The calm breeze of the water makes its way up to you, and it's pleasant.

The sky is perfectly still and of a beautiful blue colour all over.

The sun is filling you up with hope and tranquility. The colours of the sun rejoice your body.

The smell of the fresh water from the lake touches your nose and invigorates you as you listen to the sound of the wind gushing through the trees around you. The air feels like a cool, gentle touch on your skin, making you tremble with joy and positivity. You feel wonderful when the sun rays reach your hands, feet and face. Hearing the different birds around you and the wind softly going through the trees adds to your relaxation and calmness.

You start going deeper and deeper into calmness mode, just by following the rhythm of your own breathing.

This is perfect.

With each glimpse of blue water from the lake that you see, you are one step away from all the stress, carried away into the vastity of space.

Simply stand and see how all is taken away by the water and wind.

The sun is now coming up and reveals itself with its beautiful rays across the scenery.

As it does so, you are going deeper and deeper into calmness, into relaxation and bliss, with each ray of sunlight that hits your body and evaporates any tension within you.

Everything that you've been holding on for so long is now ready to go.

You are now completely ready to become worry-free. You have all the time in the world to feel at ease with your mind and body. There is no need to ponder on the stuff that worried you before.

Follow your breath, continue to breath and keep an eye on the blue water and its soft, gentle moves, as the last remaining tensions leave your body.

Pause for 1-2 minutes

You are now walking along the path on the top of the forest hill, overlooking the lake. You are worry-free about the future. You start to see how your breath becomes softer, deeper, as you feel a sense of complete calmness inside your body. All of the stress is leaving, as you feel like you're entire negative being is leaving the body. You can see yourself from above, your thoughts and emotions.

You do this just as the sun reflects the water of the lake, in its complete blue beauty.

There are no ripples in the water.

You feel calm and relaxed because of the scenery.

As you move along the path, there's a single blanket somewhere on the grass.

You are moving along, slowly reaching the blanket.

Sitting on the blanket, you realise it is extremely comfortable.

The material is of perfect texture and softness, as you lay down in a lotus position, supporting your arms on your bent knees.

The feeling of calmness is even more powerful now.

Your mind is thinking about calmness, joy, bliss, happiness and peace.

The mind transports you from a world of struggle to a place where everything you want is possible.

You can imagine a place that's completely new, or a place that you've been to before.

Simply imagine yourself travelling to the first place that pops up.

Your consciousness is taking you to places you've been to before or imagining, the critical part of the mind that has the power to do anything that you want from it being clearly more powerful than the part that says you can't do something.

If this happens, simply focus on visualising the place which first came to mind.

The very first place that you thought about is backed up by your subconscious.

The place is deeply rooted within you, and for good reasons, because it brings up that sense of true calmness, at a totally different level than anything else, a sense of peace and light, a sense of accepting your true self just the way it is.

Take a few moments to appreciate this feeling with all that you've got.

There is nothing that can hurt you here, so notice everything that makes the place unique, safe and calm.

Imagine a beam of light coming down over you that protects you, which is bright and big enough for you to move around in it.

This beam will not stop you from seeing or hearing the things from the safe space, but makes sure no negativity may enter your being.

You can even touch the beam of light on its interior walls.

What is the colour of the beam? Is it bright yellow? Is it delightful white? Is it multicoloured?

The beam is the source of all things magical, of positivity, and the removal of negativity.

You have complete control while inside the beam of light.

The beam is now part of your own self, and every time you think about the beam of light, you feel relaxation, happiness, and self love.

These feelings will get more and more powerful over time.

The beam will make you feel stronger with each new day.

The tension and stress will begin to move away, as you will be able to remove your being from bad thoughts, as they are a false part of the mind.

No matter where you are or what you do, the safe place is there for you.

Once you're back into it, you are again protected, happy and loving.

Practice the power of the beam of light by thinking about its benefits three times each day, in the morning, at lunch and before bed. Simply relieve the feeling of safety you've felt while inside the beam for the first time.

The more you do so, the better the feelings will get allocated in the mind.

All of the positive effects of the image will get more and more powerful in the mind, until the point when they'll become a permanent part of your being.

As this becomes a new part of yourself, you will be ready to make a change in your life, which will also bring more and more positive changes to you.
For a moment, start speaking with the true self within you.

Speak to that part that contains all of your bad habits.

You are conscious that smoking is a bad habit in which you've engaged once too many times,

The mind knows this, and it also controls your habits, but never without you having the last word over it.

You are the driver in your supercar, and you have the complete command centre in your cockpit.

You have the highest level of control, you are powerful and you can decide the fate of your negative smoking habit.

On a deeper level, you realise that putting a cigarette into your mouth is the moment you decide to engage in the bad habit. That's when it starts. That is the place where it all starts, not in the mouth itself, but in the deeper mind.

Everything happens in the mind at first. Ask yourself, your true self, if this is the case, and be honest about it.

As soon as you are done with listening to this meditation today, start to develop new habits that are healthier for you.

This is you building the ground for a new and improved version of yourself.

The new you finds this opportunity attractive and totally reachable.

The beautiful, blissful, engaged you.

That part of you knows the importance of you staying healthy, away from negative habits. The new you is never smoking.

The new you quits smoking because it's not defined by the habit, the absence of it makes the new you happy.

The more you stay without a cigarette, the better you feel.

You are entering a cycle of happiness, both inside and outside of the body and mind.

Like your joy, the more you're joyful, the less the urge to smoke.

The less you smoke, the more joyful you are.

The more you feel calm, the less your urge to smoke.

The less smoke you inhale, the more relaxed you become.

The more patience you gather, the less the urge to smoke.

The less you smoke, the more calm you are.

The less you smoke, the more relaxed you are.

The more relaxed you become, the less you smoke.

Every time you remind yourself to practice these techniques, you are getting stronger, healthier, better.

You want to become healthier, stronger, and better and you know that there is that version somewhere inside yourself.

Every time you choose this version of yourself, you get to experience new bounts of joy, health and positivity.

Feeling good about who you are is the best feeling.

And the best part is, whatever happens, all you have to do to experience this and go on the healthy path is to remind yourself of the benefits of the practice, of how you're gathering power over old bad habits, changing your ways.

Now, as you are far away from a smoker, the health you once lost comes back.

Your body and mind take care of yourself in a natural way, with no help from dangerous substances that can harm you.

Each day as you are not smoking you're getting better, stronger, more patient.

Every day it makes it easier and easier to continue to live healthy, positively and practically.

A life without smoking means you are mentally ordering the body to live in peace and naturally. The body will adapt and respond in a positive way, in a true way, so listen to it honestly.

Every time you take the time to listen to your body, check with it first to make sure it is in tune with the mind.

You will slowly develop a sense of clarity and see why the smoking part of your life was a mistake.

Being present in the moment, instead of ushering the mind with smoke, is all you need for joy.

The more you exercise this present state and health, the better your body becomes used to this better self.

This will keep you as healthy as you can be, free from disease.

Picture yourself as healthy as you want to be, as the goal is now reachable.

Create a positive image of yourself in the mind, see yourself as you want to be and feel the way you feel.

Go one step deeper and see yourself with your loving family, wife and kids, all enjoying a free-from-disease life in your beautiful house.

Enjoy the people around you for longer, love and cherish them regularly.

Everything will change, including your breathing and you enjoying everything much more.

You will feel a new type of energy around you, encapsulating your entire body, just as the beam of light did as you were standing on the top of the hill earlier.

The light comes down and touches your body, warming it inside and out.

This new source of energy comes from within and carries healthy aspects.

You can imagine yourself healthy and smokeless. You haven't had a cigarette in a while, and you will never need another one.

You can achieve this all by yourself, all because of this simple change in habit you decided upon doing.

By letting go of smoking, you increased your level of happiness.

You are beginning on a positive path, and you feel just like you've always wanted to feel.

Keep your focus on this very moment, and simply enjoy it.

Pause for 1-2 minutes

The time has come to get back to the conscious mind.

Start by wiggling your fingers and toes.

Elevate yourself from the depths of the mind back into the physical world.

The blood will feel like it's coming back to your extremities.

Starting from the top of the head.

Going down the spine, the core, the middle of the body.

Start counting back from five to one, and with each digit, come back to reality a bit more,

Five. Start coming back to the conscious mind.

Four. Feel the weight in your legs and arms increasing.

Three. Start sensing the smells, sounds and feels of the place you're in.

Two. Take a deep breath.

One. Open your eyes, stretch out and enjoy the feelings you're feeling for a moment.

Stop Smoking Part 2 - A Visual Short Story

Do not listen to this audio recording while driving or operating heavy machinery. Thank you.

Welcome to this guided meditation for allowing the law of attraction to bring abundance, wealth, success, love and miracles into your life.

Now, if you haven't used a guided meditation or hypnosis tape before, it's important to know that you understand what is happening to your body throughout this recording.

When you are in the state of self-hypnosis, you are not asleep, nor are you unconscious.

You're actually very aware of your surroundings, and you can't be coerced into doing anything which you don't want to.

So don't worry about any external distractions or noises because you will soon be able to relax completely.

You are always in complete control of yourself.

I will be saying a series of prompts, you can hear the suggestions and prompts as you wish.

Just allow yourself to absorb the suggestions without thinking or trying to analyze them.

And don't worry if your mind drifts off somewhere else.

You will still gain a positive outcome from the prompts and if you find yourself focusing on other thoughts, you can slowly remind yourself to focus only on my voice and what I am saying.

And don't worry if you don't think you are "getting it" or doing it right. Especially if this is your first time. There is no right or wrong way to go about this.

Just allow yourself to feel comfortable and relaxed.

Start in a comfortable position, either sitting or laying down.

And now, begin by taking just a few deep breaths, in through your nose and out through your mouth.

Really focus your attention where you feel the breath.

For some of you, that will be your nose, for some it will be your chest, and for others, you will feel it in your belly.

Wherever that place is for you, just bring your attention to that part of your body, and breathe.

If it helps, you can count the breaths as they go.

pause for 20 seconds

If you feel your mind wandering, then just bring your attention back to the breath, and feel it coming in through the nose and out through the mouth.

And as you go into a deeper state of relaxation, you will become more receptive to the words you are hearing.

Now, as you exhale this time, I want you to visualize a tree root going through you, and anchoring itself to the earth below you.

This root is your grounding root, it helps you stay centered throughout the meditation, and will provide comfort and warmth during your experience.

It also helps you focus if you mind becomes distracted.

But for now, just really feel the root anchoring itself to the ground beneath you, and how sturdy and firm you feel in your body.

You're doing great, just allow your body to expand and keep breathing in through your nose and out through your mouth.

By allowing this cord to anchor, you can release nay negative tension by sending it along the cord, so it disperses out into the earth around you.

By doing this, the tension moves out of your body, and into the world around you.

You can release any stress, tension or anxiety at any time during this meditation by releasing it along the root, and out into the universe.

Take another deep breath.

You are becoming aware of just how relaxed you are during the process.

Of how in control of your destiny you truly are

You are in the best place you could be right now.

You are in the best place you could be right now.

You are in the best place you could be right now.

Take another deep breath.

I want you to begin consciously focusing on relaxing your muscles.

We'll start at the top of your head.

Begin to feel a soothing wave of relaxation flowing down through the very top of your head.

Feel this wave caress over the crown of your head, and around the side of your head until it touches your ears.

Feel it slowly tricking down over your eyebrows, as each bit of relaxation touches your skin.

Allow it to move around the side of your eyes, as feel your face getting slightly heavier with each moment that passes.

You are at ease and you feel completely comfortable right now.

Just allow your ears to focus in on the sound of my voice, and feel the relaxation continue to move down your body.

Your muscles may even feel like they're melting slightly, this is a good thing.

And just like ice melts under the warm sun, your muscles are melting down with this wave of relaxation.

Allow this wave to come past your jaw and down into your neck.

Through your tongue and your teeth.

If you feel slightly tingly at this point, don't worry, that's completely normal – you are relaxing your muscles and going deeper into your subconscious mind

Allow the wave of relaxation to flow down the back and front of your beck, and from your head into your upper torso and upper back.

With every breathe you take you are drifting deeper and deeper into a relaxed state.

Across your shoulders and then down into your chest and back.

You are solely focused on your body right now.

Expand your chest and back as you continue to breathe.

Allowing the wave of relaxation to reach every inch of your body.

Really feel the relaxation in your muscles and tendons of your body.

And allow this relaxation to melt your muscles just like ice on a warm summer's day.

Feel the comforting warmth of relaxation across your body.

And let it keep moving down across your body down into your elbows and arms.

And further down into your fingertips.

You might feel some tingling in your fingers, don't worry, this is completely normal.

Just let this relaxation move all over your body.

Let it spread down through your belly and into your hips.

This will open you up and allow your subconscious to receive the prompts.

Now it is just you, and my voice guiding you.

As you sink deeper and deeper into a relaxed state of mind.

Allow the wave to go down into your thighs, and then down into your lower legs.

Slowly orbiting your ankles with comfort and ease.

This wave moves down deeper and deeper as we move further.

Across your calves as it relaxes your lower leg muscles, you are truly relaxed now.

Allow it to move down through your ankles, and finally into your feet.

Watch it move across the soles of your feet, as well as the tops of them.

And finally, down into your toes.

Feel the tingling of your toes as the relaxation flows through you.

Now, you are truly primed and ready to be guided on a journey to greatness.

You can imagine your root grounding you as well.

In this position, only positive effects can occur in the next 45 minutes.

Because you have allowed yourself to relax, open up, and embrace the positive changes you are about to have come into your life.

Anything is possible for you at this point.

Anything and everything is possible.

You can overcome even your biggest challenge, no matter how insurmountable that might seem right now.

In just a few seconds, I will begin to count down from five. After this, you will transported into a new world.

A world where anything is possible, and you can make the changes you want to make in life.

And as I count down, with each number, your level of relaxation will instantly increase.

Don't fight this, don't force it, just let it happen. Here we go.

Five, keep breathing, and feel yourself sinking deeper and deeper down.

Four, you are so relaxed now.

Three, just existing and letting go. It feels so good to just let go.

Two. Getting even closer now, now, peacefully, comfortably relaxed,

And one.

Take a big deep breath into your nose. Release on your mouth, and as you do so, close your eyes gently. Imagine you're on the top of a hill with nothing but grape vines surrounding you. The temperature outside is just perfect, not too cold, not too hot.

The sky is simply perfect, having a blue colour and no clouds all around.

The sun overlooks everything from behind a fluffy, singular white cloud.

The grapes are fully ripped, the smell of the fruit makes its way to you and invigorates your entire being. You listen to the sound of the soft wind blowing through the grape leaves, making its way to you in a gentle, ideal manner. You feel the best when the sun rays reach your hands, your face and your entire body. You can distinguish the sounds of birds flying over you and the sounds of the wind, which make you calm and relaxed.

Begin the practice by taking notice of how you go into more and more relaxation, by noticing the gentle breathing of your body.

You are doing good.

Every time you gaze upon the neverending green hills, you are taking one more step away from bad thoughts, stress and anxiety.

All of your worries are blown away by the wind, the sun and the vastity of space.

The sun is at the top of its day and shines its rays upon the landscape.

The more you gaze upon the beauty of the scene in front of you, the calmer you become, the more relaxed your body feels and the more at peace with everything around you.

You are now ready to let go of any emotions, thoughts or feelings you've been holding on to.

This is your time to become free from worry. This is your time to come at peace with the mind and the body. It is the best time to let go of stress and worries, forever.

Follow the rhythm of your breath, keep breathing slowly while you gaze upon the green hills and how the grape leaves move calmly when the wind blows upon them.

Pause for 2 minutes

You are now beginning a walk along a linear path at the top of the hill. There are no more worries inside you about anything while you do so.

The very breath that gives your body power is now deeper, softer, gentler. The calmness in your body overwhelms you. There is no more anxiety or stress. The whole negative aspect of your being is gone. You can see them leaving your body, both thoughts and emotions of despair.

You are free from worry as the sun is free from all earthly bounds.

The perfect green hills are your canvas.

You feel a sense of relaxation and calmness looking at this natural painting.

You reach a wooden bench somewhere along the path.

You sit on the bench and feel its rigid form, awakening the entire body.

The bench is comfortable and gives you a sense of safety.

You sit down and relax your hands into your lap, while your head is held up high and you see the entire grape vines bellow.

The calmness intensifies as you do so.

The mind is envisioning joy, happiness, relaxation and peacefulness.

Your own mind takes you and transfers you from a world of pain to a place where anything is possible.

Imagine in your mind a place where you've been before and enjoyed.

Use the mind to see yourself there, at the first place that you think about.

The mind has the ability to show you places you've enjoyed and felt safe in. Let the part of the mind that does this take over, taking you to a place where safety and joy are on the menu every single second of the day for you.

Visualise the place in your mind, see it, feel it, touch it calmly and completely.

Your favourite place is the very first that shows up, as it stays in your subconscious mind.

It has a meaning to you. It means you feel at home there, you feel safe and free from worry, from fear and bad emotions. It overflows you with calmness, more than any other place in the world, with peace and acceptance.

Breathe deeply and appreciate this feeling for a moment.

Nothing and nobody can hurt you while you sit there. Take notice of all the things that make this place safe and unique for you.

Imagine a gust of wind flowing over you like a cone. It's a soft breeze, but one that protects you from everything from the outside.

The flow of wind envelopes your body and keeps you safe, while allowing you to still feel and hear everything from the outside.

You can feel the wind blowing softly on your entire body.

What is the sensation the cone of wind gives you? How does it look? Is it flowing from the top or from the bottom of your body?

This wind is the source of your calmness, positivity and the cure of all that is negative.

While inside the cone of wind, you are in complete control.

The wind is now part of your body. The moment you think about the gentle blow of wind, you are turning into a relaxed, happy and self-loving human being.

These feelings will get more and more powerful over time.

The calm wind will make you feel stronger with each new day that passes.

The tension and stress will begin to melt away, as you will be able to remove any bad thoughts, as you realise they are a negative part of the mind.

No matter where you are or what you do, the safe place is there for you.

Once you're back into it, you are again protected, happy and loving.

Practice the power of the cone of wind by thinking about its benefits. Do this three times each day, in the morning, after lunch and right before bed. Simply recall the feeling of safety you've felt while inside the wind cone for the first time.

The more practice this, the better the thoughts and feelings of joy will get enveloped in the mind.

The positive effects of the images will get more and more intense in your mind, until one day they'll become a permanent part of you.

Now take a moment to start speaking with your true self.

More importantly, start speaking to that part of you which has all the bad habits.

You know that smoking is a bad habit.

The mind knows it and it controls all habits, good or bad, but you are the one who ultimately decides.

You are always the captain of the boat, you are in command of the vessel.

There is nobody inside you that has more control than yourself.

Deep down inside you know how bad smoking is and has been for you. It all starts with the simple act of lighting a cigarette. But it also starts in the mind at that moment, not just in the physical world.

All that we do, we do it first in the mind.

By the time you'll be done with the meditation practice, you will be ready to start working on some new habits for your benefit.

You are now building the foundation for a better version of you as a being.

You love the new opening and possibility for change.

You are now joyful, engaged, ready.

Your entire being knows how important it is for you to be healthy and stay safe from bad habits that can ruin your body and mind.

The new version of yourself is not a smoker.

The new version of yourself quits smoking now, because the habit is useless for the new you.

The more time you spend without smoking, the happier you are.

The circle of joyfulness you're about to enter is unbreakable.

The more joyful you are, the less the need to smoke becomes.

The less you feel like smoking, the more joyful you are.

The more calmer you feel, the less you need to smoke.

The less you smoke, the calmer you become.

The more you practice this circle, the better you become as a being.

With every time you practice this meditation, the better you become at health, happiness and life itself.

This is your real version, the true you, happy, strong, healthy and free from smoking.

You can choose this version of yourself every second of every minute of every hour of the day. And the more you do so, the happier you become.

Being at peace with yourself is the best thing you can do.

Simply remind yourself about the benefits of this practice every time you feel like you're about to step out of your cone of wind, of your calm and happy place. Gather courage and power over negative habits, change your strategies and move on.

You are now an ex-smoker, which has health and happiness as his priorities.

You don't need help from bad substances for you to feel good, you can achieve that naturally.

You are better, you are stronger, you are healthier with each cigarette you're not lightning.

The practice becomes more and more easy by each day.

You don't need smoking. You just need to be firm and tell your mind and body to leave naturally and at peace with whatever happens in life. Your body will follow the mind and adapt.

Make time to listen to the body, check up on it every occasion you have and tune it with the mind.

You will begin to see things more clearly, to be more aware of everything around you.

Be present in the now, remove the part of your mind that wants to get smoked away.

Exercise the practice of mindful presence every second of every day. You will become better at it the more you do it.

Being in the present will keep you on top of your life and health.

Being present will allow for the people around you to enjoy your presence for years and years, as so will you enjoy them.

Get ready for a complete change, for better breathing and for enjoying everything at a higher level.

There's going to be a new vibe, a new energy enveloping you, your entire being and body, just as the flow of wind does whenever you're bringing it up.

The cool wind calms your body down as it touches it.

The new energy source is within you, warming your being from the inside out.

Imagine this new you without the bad habit of smoking. You can't remember when you've had your last cigarette.

You don't need another one ever again.

You can live this beautiful life by yourself, with just these simple habit changes.

Let go of the ugly habit of smoking.

Increase your happiness naturally.

Get on the good path of life, feel your best, the best you've ever felt.

Enjoy every second you have on Earth to its fullest.

Pause for 1-2 minutes

Get back to your conscious mind and thinking.

Remove yourself by moving your fingers and toes gently at first.

Get back from the deepest places in your mind into the world around you.

Feel the sensations of touch coming back to your body.

Begin by checking up the top of the head first.

Go down on the spine, the stomach, the pelvis area, top and bottom of your legs.

Countdown from five to one and get back to the here while you're doing so.

Five. Elevate yourself from the subconscious to the conscious mind.

Four. Feel the weight of the body as you do so.

Three. Smell the things around you, hear the sounds in the room or wherever you are sited.

Two. Take a deep breath in through the nose, out through the mouth.

One. Open your eyes. You are back a better you, a joyful being with a better set of habits.

Overcome Addiction to Food and Lose Weight - A Visual short story

Do not listen to this audio recording while driving or operating heavy machinery. Thank you.

Welcome to this guided meditation for allowing the law of attraction to bring abundance, wealth, success, love and miracles into your life.

Now, if you haven't used a guided meditation or hypnosis tape before, it's important to know that you understand what is happening to your body throughout this recording.

When you are in the state of self-hypnosis, you are not asleep, nor are you unconscious.

You're actually very aware of your surroundings, and you can't be coerced into doing anything which you don't want to.

So don't worry about any external distractions or noises because you will soon be able to relax completely.

You are always in complete control of yourself.

I will be saying a series of prompts, you can hear the suggestions and prompts as you wish.

Just allow yourself to absorb the suggestions without thinking or trying to analyze them.

And don't worry if your mind drifts off somewhere else.

You will still gain a positive outcome from the prompts and if you find yourself focusing on other thoughts, you can slowly remind yourself to focus only on my voice and what I am saying.

And don't worry if you don't think you are "getting it" or doing it right. Especially if this is your first time. There is no right or wrong way to go about this.

Just allow yourself to feel comfortable and relaxed.

Start in a comfortable position, either sitting or laying down.

And now, begin by taking just a few deep breaths, in through your nose and out through your mouth.

Really focus your attention where you feel the breath.

For some of you, that will be your nose, for some it will be your chest, and for others, you will feel it in your belly.

Wherever that place is for you, just bring your attention to that part of your body, and breathe.

If it helps, you can count the breaths as they go.

pause for 20 seconds

If you feel your mind wandering, then just bring your attention back to the breath, and feel it coming in through the nose and out through the mouth.

And as you go into a deeper state of relaxation, you will become more receptive to the words you are hearing.

Now, as you exhale this time, I want you to visualize a tree root going through you, and anchoring itself to the earth below you.

This root is your grounding root, it helps you stay centered throughout the meditation, and will provide comfort and warmth during your experience.

It also helps you focus if you mind becomes distracted.

But for now, just really feel the root anchoring itself to the ground beneath you, and how sturdy and firm you feel in your body.

You're doing great, just allow your body to expand and keep breathing in through your nose and out through your mouth.

By allowing this cord to anchor, you can release nay negative tension by sending it along the cord, so it disperses out into the earth around you.

By doing this, the tension moves out of your body, and into the world around you.

You can release any stress, tension or anxiety at any time during this meditation by releasing it along the root, and out into the universe.

Take another deep breath.

You are becoming aware of just how relaxed you are during the process.

Of how in control of your destiny you truly are

You are in the best place you could be right now.

You are in the best place you could be right now.

You are in the best place you could be right now.

Take another deep breath.

I want you to begin consciously focusing on relaxing your muscles.

We'll start at the top of your head.

Begin to feel a soothing wave of relaxation flowing down through the very top of your head.

Feel this wave caress over the crown of your head, and around the side of your head until it touches your ears.

Feel it slowly tricking down over your eyebrows, as each bit of relaxation touches your skin.

Allow it to move around the side of your eyes, as feel your face getting slightly heavier with each moment that passes.

You are at ease and you feel completely comfortable right now.

Just allow your ears to focus in on the sound of my voice, and feel the relaxation continue to move down your body.

Your muscles may even feel like they're melting slightly, this is a good thing.

And just like ice melts under the warm sun, your muscles are melting down with this wave of relaxation.

Allow this wave to come past your jaw and down into your neck.

Through your tongue and your teeth.

If you feel slightly tingly at this point, don't worry, that's completely normal – you are relaxing your muscles and going deeper into your subconscious mind

Allow the wave of relaxation to flow down the back and front of your beck, and from your head into your upper torso and upper back.

With every breathe you take you are drifting deeper and deeper into a relaxed state.

Across your shoulders and then down into your chest and back.

You are solely focused on your body right now.

Expand your chest and back as you continue to breathe.

Allowing the wave of relaxation to reach every inch of your body.

Really feel the relaxation in your muscles and tendons of your body.

And allow this relaxation to melt your muscles just like ice on a warm summer's day.

Feel the comforting warmth of relaxation across your body.

And let it keep moving down across your body down into your elbows and arms.

And further down into your fingertips.

You might feel some tingling in your fingers, don't worry, this is completely normal.

Just let this relaxation move all over your body.

Let it spread down through your belly and into your hips.

This will open you up and allow your subconscious to receive the prompts.

Now it is just you, and my voice guiding you.

As you sink deeper and deeper into a relaxed state of mind.

Allow the wave to go down into your thighs, and then down into your lower legs.

Slowly orbiting your ankles with comfort and ease.

This wave moves down deeper and deeper as we move further.

Across your calves as it relaxes your lower leg muscles, you are truly relaxed now.

Allow it to move down through your ankles, and finally into your feet.

Watch it move across the soles of your feet, as well as the tops of them.

And finally, down into your toes.

Feel the tingling of your toes as the relaxation flows through you.

Now, you are truly primed and ready to be guided on a journey to greatness.

You can imagine your root grounding you as well.

In this position, only positive effects can occur in the next 45 minutes.

Because you have allowed yourself to relax, open up, and embrace the positive changes you are about to have come into your life.

Anything is possible for you at this point.

Anything and everything is possible.

You can overcome even your biggest challenge, no matter how insurmountable that might seem right now.

In just a few seconds, I will begin to count down from five. After this, you will transported into a new world.

A world where anything is possible, and you can make the changes you want to make in life.

And as I count down, with each number, your level of relaxation will instantly increase.

Don't fight this, don't force it, just let it happen. Here we go.

Five, keep breathing, and feel yourself sinking deeper and deeper down.

Four, you are so relaxed now.

Three, just existing and letting go. It feels so good to just let go.

Two. Getting even closer now, now, peacefully, comfortably relaxed,

And one.

Scenario - Snow capped mountain valley

Take a moment to relax and settle down. Close your eyes and imagine yourself in a beautiful, green valley surrounded by snow capped mountains. The sun is up and bright, the day is perfectly warm and the breeze of the wind is ideal.

The sky is a perfect blue colour, with small white clouds here and there.

The sun is up in the sky, warming everything that it touches.

The smell of the mountain air is undeniably a hard one, but a healing one. The soft wind touches your skin and cools you off as you listen to the sounds of the valley. You feel ready to relax, and with every breath that you take, you become calmer and more open to a change in your life. A change that will make you a better human being.

You begin to go deeper and deeper into relaxation mode, following your gentle breath as you do so.

Perfect.

With each fluffy cloud that comes into your view, you let go of the stress in your body, the tension goes away into the vast universe.

Simply stay there and see the tension move away into the clouds.

The sun rays flow towards you, beautiful orange rays covering the entire green valley.

As they do so, the entire being of you is going deeper and deeper into calmness and comfort, with each cloud that moves above you into the skies.

The stress that you have left inside you is ready to depart now.

This is the perfect time for you to become relaxed and aware of everything around you. Become at ease with the elements, the earth and the air and the snow and the sun rays.

Follow your breathing for a minute or two, as you notice every little cloud in the sky passing along the gorgeous scenery, taking away any stressors you might have in the body.

Pause for 1 minute

Imagine yourself taking a walk along a path into the valley. As you move along, the worries you've had until now start to dissipate.

Breathe in and out calmly, noticing how the breath becomes deeper, but softer and as calmness enters your body from the outside and stress leaving it from the inside.

As the cloud reflects its own clouds and beauty, so you can reflect your own slef.

The calmness of the scenery is entering your body and mind.

In the perfectly cool valley, somewhere along the path you see a small math.

Move towards the math with ease.

Sit on the math in a cross-legged position which feels comfortable.

The body supports its entire weight with no effort as you do so. Everything is comfortable.

Feel your entire being sinking into the math and drifting away into more relaxation and good mood. Peace is overflowing your mind, comfort and light and happiness.

Allow your mind to imagine a new place where anything is entirely possible.

It doesn't matter if you've been to this place before or not, simply let the mind transport you there.

Travel to the first place that comes to mind.

It might take a while for the mind to decide on a place. Take your time, don't rush anything, there's plenty of minutes to spare.

The conscious being that you are playing with the subconscious mind, the mind that thinks and acts, the mind that says what you can and cannot do.

Regardless of your thoughts, don't worry on anything but just focus on the very first image that pops into your conscious mind.

This first place you're seeing is important to you.

It comes from deep within you and for a good reason, as this might be one of the very places where you feel at home, safe and relaxed as nowhere else, where you feel happy, joyful, comfortable and alive, where you accept your entire being just the way it is.

Take a few seconds to enjoy these powerful feelings with every sense that you've got.

Notice the things that make the place special, safe and relaxing.

Now, imagine a large protective dome of light coming down above you. You can move around into it and breathe with ease.

The dome of light will not deprive you off sounds and the scenery of your safe place, but makes everything safe and removes all negative things.

You can touch the dome on its edges and move around it for a moment.

Describe the dome in your mind, its shape, size, colour and even smell.

The best part about the dome is, this is a place of positivity and a remover of all that is negative.

You are in complete control in the dome, about everything that stays or leaves.

The dome is now part of your own self. As soon as you think about it, your mind will think about joy, happiness and safety.

The feelings associated with the dome of light will get stronger with time.

You will feel more positivity day after day, as you imagine the dome over you.

All negativity and stress will fade away, as will your bad thoughts and memories of the past, as these are no longer part of the real you.

The dome, which is your safe place, will be there for you at all times.

The moment you step back into the light dome, you will be filled with happiness, self love and surrounded by a protective medium.

Practice these feelings every single day by imagining yourself back into your dome. The more times you do it, the more natural it becomes for you to feel protected and loved.

Your mind will associate you thinking about the dome with a pleasant state, so it will become easier to achieve the state of joy you deserve.

All of the benefits of this positive, self accepting image and even more important is that each time the concept and images become more permanently fixed in your mind.

And when they are there, you know will activate a positive change in your life, which then snowballs into more positive changes for you.

It is now time to talk to your deep self and more importantly, about your eating habits.

The body needs just as much food to survive, which you've neglected in the past.

Your mind is aware of this.

Although the mind tells you what and when to eat, you are the one who's driving the mind after all.

Imagine the mind being a joystick from a gaming console. You look at all the buttons and knobs.

From now on, you are the player who's deciding what you can and cannot do, what is good and what is bad for you, your mind and your body.

From this moment forward, you are deciding consciously the type and quantity of food you put in your mouth. Discovering this new power that you have over your urges, you go deeper and deeper into your true self and make this a permanent change, eating mindfully, not by what the stomach tells you to.

Everything is in the mind, if you're being really honest and look inside for a moment.

The time has come to set some goals from today on and stick to them as soon as this practice comes to an end.

These are the first few bricks of the foundation that will become the new, better you.

The more you think about these changes, the better they look for you.

Everything feels right, wonderful and happy.

Health is a subject you've always cherished and tried to keep on top of things. The new you is simply healthy by default.

Simply by eating the right things, there's some chemical magic happening into you.

The better you feel, the smaller the urge to eat will be.

The levels of your inner and outer happiness will increase.

The more you feel great, the less you'll eat.

The less you eat, the better you'll feel.

The more you feel calm, the less you eat.

The less you eat, the calmer you'll be.

Here's another one, which is hard to grasp, but stay with me.

The less you eat, the more powerful you become.

The more power you have, the less you eat.

Every time you practice this meditation session, you are getting healthier, better, slimmer, more powerful and self-loving.

Your true self always wants to be slim, healthy, energetic and better than the actual version of yourself.

Every time you make a good eating choice, the new you is happy, excited and calm.

The feelings that the new you has are perfect.

Simply repeat these new healthy habits every single day for the best version of yourself.

Run every single day for a better understanding of how it feels to be strong and happy. See how the pleasures for everything, even exercise, grow stronger with each day you're doing the practice.

Change the relationship you have with food. Eat naturally, better and healthier foods, in order to become more and more relaxed and happy about who you are.

With each day that you do these things, you're getting better and better at eating right.

Every day, it gets easier to keep this practice going, in a positive way.

Eating healthy is nothing more than asking the body what it wants to consume, and your body naturally asking for great foods that will nourish and strengthen its core foundation.

The moment you take some time to listen to your body quietly, you will be able to understand it better and better with each listening.

You will slowly begin to understand why the body needs to stay healthy and how food is important to be consumed slowly and gently.

You will notice how savouring the flavours of the food, concentrating on every mouthful, is so important.

Being present for every single bite.

It will help you get down to the weight you've always wanted to have.

Picture yourself as you've always wanted to look like in the mind.

By creating this positive image of yourself in the mind, just as you'd want to look like, you're putting your entire being at work for creating that self you desire.

Go one step further and dress yourself in the clothes you've always wanted. Experience the good looks feelings that image brings you.

Imagine yourself truly enjoying running more. The more you do it, the better you become at it.

Breathing calmly while doing your runs will get you to enjoy workouts more.

Feeling good about moving will become a new part of your healthier version, being fit will become a new staple in your life, using the energy you get for the better will become your reason to get up and do sports on a daily basis.

As you engage in sporting activities more and more, you will feel an overflow of positivity and energy running through your body with each workout.

Once again, feel the breeze of fresh mountain air touching your skin.

The air which brings you life carries energy around, energy allowing you to set up new, better habits.

Picture this energy transferring into your willingness to change, to become slimmer and better.

Visualize your bathroom scale, see the number that you've always wanted to see on the display.

It's right there, isn't it?

This is all you, you're capable of this.

How do you feel right at this moment?

This is all your achievement, all because the small, but strict changes you've made in daily habits.

Eating less.

Moving more.

Being happier as a base for all things.

The new level of positivity you've reached is undeniable, as you see yourself in the mirror, just how you've always dreamed of looking. Sit with this image for a moment or so.

Pause for 2 minutes

The time has come for you to get back in the conscious world.

Start by moving your toes slowly. Move to the fingers.

Rise back up into the conscious mind.

Have your head inspected for a moment, notice the sensations in it.

Go down on the spine, neck, back, chest and stomach, continuing all the way down towards the feet.

As you reach the bottom of your body, you will feel warm, calm, healed, changed, better.

Five. Start by gazing upon the conscious part of the mind.

Four. Feel the sensations in your entire body coming back to normal.

Three. Notice the sensations around you, in your room, being sounds, smells or both.

Two. Get ready to fully come back now.

One. Open your eyes gently, stretch out and appreciate what you've just done.

Overcome Addiction to Food and Lose Weight Part 2 - A Visual Short Story

Do not listen to this audio recording while driving or operating heavy machinery. Thank you.

Welcome to this guided meditation for allowing the law of attraction to bring abundance, wealth, success, love and miracles into your life.

Now, if you haven't used a guided meditation or hypnosis tape before, it's important to know that you understand what is happening to your body throughout this recording.

When you are in the state of self-hypnosis, you are not asleep, nor are you unconscious.

You're actually very aware of your surroundings, and you can't be coerced into doing anything which you don't want to.

So don't worry about any external distractions or noises because you will soon be able to relax completely.

You are always in complete control of yourself.

I will be saying a series of prompts, you can hear the suggestions and prompts as you wish.

Just allow yourself to absorb the suggestions without thinking or trying to analyze them.

And don't worry if your mind drifts off somewhere else.

You will still gain a positive outcome from the prompts and if you find yourself focusing on other thoughts, you can slowly remind yourself to focus only on my voice and what I am saying.

And don't worry if you don't think you are "getting it" or doing it right. Especially if this is your first time. There is no right or wrong way to go about this.

Just allow yourself to feel comfortable and relaxed.

Start in a comfortable position, either sitting or laying down.

And now, begin by taking just a few deep breaths, in through your nose and out through your mouth.

Really focus your attention where you feel the breath.

For some of you, that will be your nose, for some it will be your chest, and for others, you will feel it in your belly.

Wherever that place is for you, just bring your attention to that part of your body, and breathe.

If it helps, you can count the breaths as they go.

pause for 20 seconds

If you feel your mind wandering, then just bring your attention back to the breath, and feel it coming in through the nose and out through the mouth.

And as you go into a deeper state of relaxation, you will become more receptive to the words you are hearing.

Now, as you exhale this time, I want you to visualize a tree root going through you, and anchoring itself to the earth below you.

This root is your grounding root, it helps you stay centered throughout the meditation, and will provide comfort and warmth during your experience.

It also helps you focus if you mind becomes distracted.

But for now, just really feel the root anchoring itself to the ground beneath you, and how sturdy and firm you feel in your body.

You're doing great, just allow your body to expand and keep breathing in through your nose and out through your mouth.

By allowing this cord to anchor, you can release nay negative tension by sending it along the cord, so it disperses out into the earth around you.

By doing this, the tension moves out of your body, and into the world around you.

You can release any stress, tension or anxiety at any time during this meditation by releasing it along the root, and out into the universe.

Take another deep breath.

You are becoming aware of just how relaxed you are during the process.

Of how in control of your destiny you truly are

You are in the best place you could be right now.

You are in the best place you could be right now.

You are in the best place you could be right now.

Take another deep breath.

I want you to begin consciously focusing on relaxing your muscles.

We'll start at the top of your head.

Begin to feel a soothing wave of relaxation flowing down through the very top of your head.

Feel this wave caress over the crown of your head, and around the side of your head until it touches your ears.

Feel it slowly tricking down over your eyebrows, as each bit of relaxation touches your skin.

Allow it to move around the side of your eyes, as feel your face getting slightly heavier with each moment that passes.

You are at ease and you feel completely comfortable right now.

Just allow your ears to focus in on the sound of my voice, and feel the relaxation continue to move down your body.

Your muscles may even feel like they're melting slightly, this is a good thing.

And just like ice melts under the warm sun, your muscles are melting down with this wave of relaxation.

Allow this wave to come past your jaw and down into your neck.

Through your tongue and your teeth.

If you feel slightly tingly at this point, don't worry, that's completely normal – you are relaxing your muscles and going deeper into your subconscious mind

Allow the wave of relaxation to flow down the back and front of your beck, and from your head into your upper torso and upper back.

With every breathe you take you are drifting deeper and deeper into a relaxed state.

Across your shoulders and then down into your chest and back.

You are solely focused on your body right now.

Expand your chest and back as you continue to breathe.

Allowing the wave of relaxation to reach every inch of your body.

Really feel the relaxation in your muscles and tendons of your body.

And allow this relaxation to melt your muscles just like ice on a warm summer's day.

Feel the comforting warmth of relaxation across your body.

And let it keep moving down across your body down into your elbows and arms.

And further down into your fingertips.

You might feel some tingling in your fingers, don't worry, this is completely normal.

Just let this relaxation move all over your body.

Let it spread down through your belly and into your hips.

This will open you up and allow your subconscious to receive the prompts.

Now it is just you, and my voice guiding you.

As you sink deeper and deeper into a relaxed state of mind.

Allow the wave to go down into your thighs, and then down into your lower legs.

Slowly orbiting your ankles with comfort and ease.

This wave moves down deeper and deeper as we move further.

Across your calves as it relaxes your lower leg muscles, you are truly relaxed now.

Allow it to move down through your ankles, and finally into your feet.

Watch it move across the soles of your feet, as well as the tops of them.

And finally, down into your toes.

Feel the tingling of your toes as the relaxation flows through you.

Now, you are truly primed and ready to be guided on a journey to greatness.

You can imagine your root grounding you as well.

In this position, only positive effects can occur in the next 45 minutes.

Because you have allowed yourself to relax, open up, and embrace the positive changes you are about to have come into your life.

Anything is possible for you at this point.

Anything and everything is possible.

You can overcome even your biggest challenge, no matter how insurmountable that might seem right now.

In just a few seconds, I will begin to count down from five. After this, you will transported into a new world.

A world where anything is possible, and you can make the changes you want to make in life.

And as I count down, with each number, your level of relaxation will instantly increase.

Don't fight this, don't force it, just let it happen. Here we go.

Five, keep breathing, and feel yourself sinking deeper and deeper down.

Four, you are so relaxed now.

Three, just existing and letting go. It feels so good to just let go.

Two. Getting even closer now, now, peacefully, comfortably relaxed,

And one.

It's the middle of Spring and you find yourself in a beautiful, calm, quiet lavender field. You are surrounded by smells, sounds of birds and insects, sights of nothing but purple flowers and sensations of peace. The temperature is ideal, as the sun comes up from beneath the Earth.

The sun is a beautiful orange color, its rays coming down on your skin, warming it up all over.

The sky is without a single cloud, in a perfect blue color.

The taste you get in your mouth is of freshness, green and purple, grass, coolness, and as you listen to the soft wind going through the infinite field of lavender, you feel the smell of the flowers invigorating you in many ways, making you more awake and aware of everything surrounding you, letting you feel the beauty of your surroundings.

The more you smell the flowers, the deeper you go into relaxation, following your gentle, soft breathing.

Perfect, you are doing great.

With each gust of wind touching the lavender, you can feel how another part of your stressful being is lifted and removed from the body.

The tension floats away with every smell of flowers you can sense with the nose.

The sun is now beginning to reach even higher ground, spreading its rays all over the field of flowers.

As it does so, you feel yourself going into even more relaxation and comfort, with each light beam coming down and then up again carrying your tension and stress away.

The remaining tension you've got left is now ready to depart.

Within a few moments, you realise this is the time for you to turn a new page into your life's story book and completely relax at the idea of change, never worried about the past.

Take all the time that you need. Keep breathing gently and notice the lavender patches blowing softly in the wind, carrying away the last remaining balls of tension from the body.

Breathe for 2 minutes

Begin walking through the lavender field in whichever way you want. The things that worried you yesterday stopped worrying you now.

You feel like you can almost sit above your own body, looking down and seeing a peaceful, relaxed, calm being, as you continue to breathe, with each breath becoming softer, deeper and more enjoyable, you can see your mind getting better at just sitting there, doing nothing.

Just as you can stare at the sea of flowers in front of you, you can see your mind at ease.

The landscape gets you calmer and calmer with every breath.

As you move along the path gently, you can see a tiny grass circle somewhere.

Moving towards the grass, you feel more and more relaxed.

You sit on the grass and realise it is comfortable.

The soft grass is perfect, the coolness of it is ideal, the body feels great sitting on it, touching it, feeling it.

You begin to sink even further into calmness, safety and relaxation.

You begin to think about health, safety, freedom and goodness.

Your mind transports you to a place where everything is doable, possible, manageable.

It doesn't matter if this is somewhere new or somewhere you've been to before.

Pick the very first spot it shows up in the mind.

Wherever the spot is on the planet, it just shows how important it is for you as it was the first thing to pop up into your conscious existence, as the thinking part of the mind did all the work of the subconscious part of the mind without any judgements.

Simply focus on the spot that your mind has picked up for you.

This very first place that popped up in the mind is one backed up by the subconscious.

On a deeper level, the spot is associated in the mind with safety, authenticity, health and wellbeing, with true bliss, happiness, calmness and perfect comfort and light and all that is good and positive for you in your life.

Take a few moments to notice and appreciate the place you're now in its entirety.

What makes the place safe, what makes the place secure, what makes the place the spot where nothing can harm you.

Now, imagine a large beam of purple light coming down around you, big so that it can envelop you but allow you to breathe calmly.

This beam of light will not block your touch with the outside world, but still let you listen to the sounds, feel the air and smell the smells.

Simply stand up and move towards the edges of the beam of light, touching them gently.

What is the color of the dome exactly, how do you perceive it?

The beam of purple light is enhanced with the ability to remove negativity and bring positivity.

The one in control while inside the beam is entirely you, about what comes in or goes out.

The beam of light is becoming a part of your own being. As soon as it happens, you will associate it with light, self love, health and blissfulness.

These feelings will get more and more powerful with time, allowing you to say no to negativity in a heartbeat.

The stress and plus weight you were having in the past will fade away, as you will be able to remove negative thought patterns as they're no longer part of you.

This is from now on your safe place.

Every time you come back to the safe place, you will be protected, loved and happy.

Every time you'll practice visualising this image of the beam of purple light, for as many times as you want each day, you will get better at enveloping these feelings and emotions of joy and happiness.

Joy, happiness and calmness will all become imprinted in your mind, day after day, becoming easier to reach and activate.

This new image of a positive and self accepting you will become stronger and stronger within you with each time you'll practice seeing it in the mind.

A positive change in your life comes every time you activate this mindful image inside your mind, which grows and grows with each activation.

It is now time to go one level further within and speak to the self directly.

In this inside part, you will find the place where bad eating habits are stored.

You are aware of the fact that you've been stress-eating way too much in the past.

Your mind and body knows this.

The mind controls everything, including eating, with you in the background as an overviewer.

You control the mind that controls everything about it, so if you look honestly at it, you do all the work. You are in control of all that goes in and comes out, including what you eat, when you eat, how much you eat, all eating habits that you have.

All that you put in the mouth, all the food that you consume, even if it doesn't feel like it, you are in control of how much you eat. You are now in with your deeper self. This is not your stomach, but the very centre of your being that controls metabolism, appetite and what you consume.

Everything happens in the mind first, so be honest and ask the deeper you the questions you need to.

The second this practice ends, you are ready to develop new, better eating habits for your being and start becoming positive about change.

You are at this very moment founding your new true, positive self.

The goal you're setting seems reachable and attractive for the new you.

The new self is happy, truthful, blissful and courageous.

The new you knows how you can become a better, healthier being, a more active and beautiful being, as the new you needs less food.

Simply by eating less, you can start to see the magic happening because the less you consume, the better you feel.

The better you feel, the less you need to eat.

The more you laugh, the less you have to eat.

The less you feel the need to eat, the more you laugh.

The more relaxed you become, the less food you need.

The less food you need, the more relaxed you become.

The more time you spend away from food, the less you eat.

The less you eat, the easier it is to stay away from food.

Every single time you're practicing this meditative session, remember you are on your way to becoming fit, healthy, happy and naturally better.

The new you is slim, energetic, filled with joy and wellbeing, health and all that is good.

Every time you choose to be the new you, to see the image of the new you, you feel healthy and calm and positive.

It feels awesome to feel this way, to be the new you.

Simply repeat these healthy patterns every day for maximum effect on the long term. You are getting stronger and stronger by doing so and your powers over bad food enhance, as you will get more satisfied the better you eat.

You will also feel the urge to go to the gym, as these new strengths of the body will help you along the way. The strength grows every single day and you will become better at sports.

Your new eating habits are healthy and more sensible, and these habits are more and more at hand for you.

As you eat more mindfully, you become better at it and stronger at the core.

Going like this in a practical and healthy way becomes naturally with each new day.

Eating in a healthy way is when you mentally ask your body for the nutrients it needs. The body tells you exactly what you want to hear, but only if you listen to it with intent and honesty.

Take your time, listen to the body with calm and complete commitment, check with the body before you eat.

Are you hungry or not? Understand your body before anything else. Eat when needed, do it slowly and calmly.

Savor the food, enjoy eating for the pleasure of it, not for stuffing your stomach with it, be there for every bite and mouthful.

The body loves the new, healthy pattern you're on now, as it is easier for it to keep up with eating healthy and good exercise.

You can be at the weight you've always wanted to be at now.

Simply use your new ability to get in touch with the true self.

Imagine your body being at the weight you want right now.

Structure a mental image, a positive one, about what you want to look like and how you'd feel about it.

Go one small step further, pick up your favourite clothes that never fit you and dress with them. Wear them, see how they'd fit you perfectly and how good you look.

Like this, your motivation for exercise and good eating will get stronger and stronger.

You will become a better executor, a more courageous breather in your workouts.

You feel awesome when you work out and healthier with each mile that you run, you enjoy seeing the healthier version, the fit version of yourself, your new energy and positivity.

The new energy that you have spreads around you like a dome of power, flows through the body like sun rays you've seen earlier in the lavender fields.

The energy flows and touches your arms and legs, warming the inside and outsite.

With this new energy, you are able to enhance the new eating habits forever.

You have achieved this all with the help of your true self, which is the healthy you, the good eating habits you, the positive you and the natural you.

You got better at eating naturally and smaller plates. That's all you.

You got better at physical activities. That's all you.

You got better at feeling happy by default. That is all you.

You are now in a positive state of mind, looking and feeling just the way you've always wanted to.

Enjoy the moment, the very moment everything makes sense, take it all in.

Breathe calmly for one minute

You are now more than ready to come back from the depths of the mind.

Begin by moving a part of your body, like the hands or the feet.

Start coming back to your conscious state of being.

Tingling will be felt in the fingers and toes at first.

Start the flow of blood from the head.

Move the blood through the neck, spine, chest, stomach, middle area, legs and all the way down to your feet.

I will now start counting from one to five. When I'll get to five, you can open the eyes.

You will feel love, health and warmness inside when that happens.

You will feel positive, energy and good thoughts.

One. Move the mind towards consciousness.

Two. Feel the weight of the hands and knees and feet.

Three. Start noticing the different sounds and smells and sensations around you.

Four. Get ready by taking one final, big breath.

Five. Open the eyes slowly. You can begin to stretch the body and enjoy the practice's end.

Powerful Self Affirmations for Weight Loss

Do not listen to this audio recording while driving or operating heavy machinery. Thank you.

Welcome to this guided meditation for allowing the law of attraction to help you lose weight, look better, feel healthier and get the best out of your life.

It is recommended you listen to this recording for 21 days straight to unlock the true power of the Law of Attraction principles.

Now, if you haven't used a guided meditation or hypnosis tape before, it's important to know that you understand what is happening to your body throughout this recording.

When you are in the state of self hypnosis, you are not asleep, nor are you unconscious.

You're actually very aware of your surroundings, and you can't be coerced into doing anything which you don't want to.

So don't worry about any external distractions or noises because you will soon be able to relax completely.

You are always in complete control of yourself.

I will be saying a series of prompts, you can hear the suggestions and prompts as you wish.

Just allow yourself to absorb the suggestions without thinking or trying to analyze them.

And don't worry if your mind drifts off somewhere else.

You will still gain a positive outcome from the prompts and if you find yourself focusing on other thoughts, you can slowly remind yourself to focus only on my voice and what I am saying.

And don't worry if you don't think you are "getting it" or doing it right. Especially if this is your first time. There is no right or wrong way to go about this.

Just allow yourself to feel comfortable and relaxed.

And begin by taking a few deep breaths.

Breathe in through your nose, and out through your mouth.

And if you want, count the breathes as they come.

So if your mind wanders, just bring your focus back the breath.

Just breath in through your nose, and out through your mouth.

Now, I will begin the affirmations which will assist you on your weight loss journey.

1. My body is strong on its own
2. I have complete control of my decisions

3. I only make healthy choices
4. I know what makes me feel good, and I choose that path every single time
5. I have complete control of my body, my mind and my spirit
6. The most important thing is how I feel in my body, regardless of the number on the scale
7. I am moving in the right direction every single day that I am alive
8. I am in control of my own destiny in all things that I do
9. I have overcome so much already in life, and I will continue to overcome everything going forward
10. I know my past decisions do not affect my future
11. My mind feels clear and my spirit feels clean every time I wake up in the morning
12. Losing weight will benefit me in so many different ways
13. I am truly a strong person and I know that I can achieve anything that I want
14. I am focused on my health because this is the most important thing in my life
15. I will move on the plane to greatness
16. This journey is teaching me so much about who I am and the priorities I have in life
17. Going forward, I will make the best decisions for my body in the long term instead of relying on instant gratification

18. I am not my mistakes, and my mistakes are not me
19. Small steps create giant leaps, and I make small steps every single day
20. When I wake up and look in the mirror, I am proud of who I am
21. By blending in, I share the same qualities as everyone else, therefore I will take my own path in this life
22. I continue to live with zero regrets in life
23. I am the greatest version of my self today, and I will continue to become greater every day
24. I continue to make good choices in life and these choices will benefit me for the rest of my days
25. I am taking care of myself now and will continue to do so in the future
26. Life is easier for me when I am making healthy choices
27. My healthy physical state moves into my healthy mental state
28. I am looking better and better every time I look into the mirror
29. I choose to spend time with people who encourage my weight loss goals and who support me on my journey to reach them.
30. Negative people have no place in my life.
31. I love how I look in the mirror from every single angle.
32. I know that I am my own weight loss transformation story and that I am in complete control of my own destiny in how my body looks and feels.

33. I am getting healthier and slimmer every single day I am alive on this Earth

34. I am a beautiful person who people love and who loves being around other beautiful people.

35. I am a joy to speak with and people who meet me love my gracious charismatic energy.

36. People always ask me how I look so good all the time, and the answer is because I feel so good all the time.

37. I am always striving to do my best in whatever form that takes.

38. Nothing can come close to how I feel when I wake up in the morning and know that I am a good person.

39. The universe is aligned with my weight loss goals.

40. I am constantly working towards an ideal version of myself.

41. It is so easy for me to make healthy choices in the kitchen.

42. I love everything I have accomplished recently.

43. I can do anything that I set my mind to.

44. I do not want unhealthy food in my life, and I will reject the temptation of it when in front of me

45. I am a stronger person who can do anything I put my mind to.

46. I can always conquer any challenge, whether that challenge is physical or mental.

47. I have no problem with working towards a long term goal.

48. Losing weight is easy for me.

49. The universe is aligned with my plans, and my plans are aligned with the universe.

50. It is important for me to understand that I am always working towards a worthy ideal.

51. I am surrounded by positive people who are a good influence on me in my life.

52. My choices in reflect who I am and who I desire to be going forward

53. I am supercharged with energy when I wake up in the morning.

54. I can move towards my goals with a ferocious speed

55. I do not want to eat food which is unhealthy for me

56. I will take the smart decisions for my long term weight loss goals

57. I always choose to surround myself with people who are supportive and whose presence in my life is beneficial to me

58. I am cool, calm and collected when I approach any situation.

59. I am always pushing myself to do better and to be the best version of myself.

60. I am a healthy person who always makes healthy choices.

61. I can overcome and succeed in any weight loss goal and my abilities will reward me when I achieve them.

62. It is with zero doubt that I know full well I can overcome any obstacles which are in front of me on my weight loss journey.
63. The universe is aligned with my goals, and I continue to see myself achieving everything I want
64. I am happy and content with who I am as a person.
65. Every day in the morning, I wake up and visualize how my days is going to go
66. I love losing weight, and I love how I feel when I am lighter
67. I can do anything which I want to in this life, and I know I have the inner strength to complete my goals

Now, it's time to return to your conscious mind.

Begin by slowly wiggling your toes, as you begin to return to the surface level.

You can feel yourself rising up back up into the conscious world.

You'll begin to feel sensation in your fingers...

At the top of your head.

And up from the base of your spine, to the top of your head.

Now, I will begin counting upwards, with each number, you will elevate your consciousness a little more.

When I reach five, you can open your eyes.

You will feel healed, loved, and warm inside.

You will feel positively energized throughout your body.

One. Moving slowly towards your conscious state.

Two. Your arms and legs will now have more weight on them.

Three. Pay attention to the room you are in, and feel the air around you.

Four. Your eyes are ready now.

Five. Open your eyes now, you can begin to stretch and enjoy what you just experienced.

Powerful Self Affirmations to Stop Smoking

Do not listen to this audio recording while driving or operating heavy machinery. Thank you.

Welcome to this guided meditation for allowing the law of attraction to help you stop smoking, look better, feel healthier and get the best out of your life.

It is recommended you listen to this recording for 21 days straight to unlock the true power of the Law of Attraction principles.

Now, if you haven't used a guided meditation or hypnosis tape before, it's important to know that you understand what is happening to your body throughout this recording.

When you are in the state of self hypnosis, you are not asleep, nor are you unconscious.

You're actually very aware of your surroundings, and you can't be coerced into doing anything which you don't want to.

So don't worry about any external distractions or noises because you will soon be able to relax completely.

You are always in complete control of yourself.

I will be saying a series of prompts, you can hear the suggestions and prompts as you wish.

Just allow yourself to absorb the suggestions without thinking or trying to analyze them.

And don't worry if your mind drifts off somewhere else.

You will still gain a positive outcome from the prompts and if you find yourself focusing on other thoughts, you can slowly remind yourself to focus only on my voice and what I am saying.

And don't worry if you don't think you are "getting it" or doing it right. Especially if this is your first time. There is no right or wrong way to go about this.

Just allow yourself to feel comfortable and relaxed.

And begin by taking a few deep breaths.

Breathe in through your nose, and out through your mouth.

And if you want, count the breathes as they come.

So if your mind wanders, just bring your focus back the breath.

Just breath in through your nose, and out through your mouth.

Now, I will begin the affirmations which will assist you on your journey to stop smoking.

1. My body is strong on its own, I do not need external chemicals to assist me

2. I am a non smoker, and I do not require cigarettes in my life
3. I love being able to walk further, run faster and accomplish more in life
4. My clothes smell fresh and clean every day
5. My teeth are looking bright white and sparkling clean
6. I am a healthy being who always chooses to do the right thing for my mind and body
7. Anything is possible for me, because I am my own biggest asset in life's journey
8. I choose to surround myself with positive influences
9. I can always do better, and I strive to reach this every day
10. Every day was less cigarettes is a move towards true freedom
11. I refuse to be held a slave to outside chemical influences, and nicotine will not change that
12. I do not require tobacco to function in daily life
13. I am a stronger person without cigarettes than I am with one
14. No thank you I would not like a cigarette, I would not like a cigarette, I would not like a cigarette,
15. I would like to sit in the non smoking section please
16. I would like a non smoking room please
17. No thanks, I don't smoke
18. I love how my body feels now that I am no longer held capture by nicotine

19. I can breathe easier every single day

20. I love going on love walks and breathing in fresh air

21. I can do anything that I set my mind to

22. I am the strongest I have every been today, and tomorrow I will be stronger still

23. I am a successful person who can do anything I want

24. I am the living embodiment of health

25. I always make good choices with my body

26. My body is a temple and I choose to fuel it with everything it needs to be primed for action

27. I love who I am, and I love who I am becoming

28. It is with great pleasure that I look in the mirror and see who is looking back at me

29. I have the universe on my side, and with this knowledge I can do anything

30. The law of attraction is with me in everything I do, and this powerful law is the force that guides me through any challenge, any struggle or any hurdle in front of me

31. Weaker people than me have reached their goals

32. I continue to strive to be the strongest version of myself

33. I become what I think about, and I am primed for success

34. Absolutely everything is possible for me in this day and age

35. With the wonders of modern technology, it is so easy for me to succeed in my goals

36. I love investing in myself, for it shows that I am somebody who is worth my weight in gold

37. I am the best version of myself I can be today, and tomorrow I will be even better still.

38. I am on an upward trajectory in life.

39. I know full well that I will stop at nothing to reach my ultimate dreams and desires.

40. I have all the tools at my disposal to live my dream life.

41. I love everyone around me, and am eternally grateful for the support and love they provide to me

42. It is so easy to be a good person, and to show love and light to those around me

43. I am a continuous positive presence in my life and the lives of others.

44. I walk my own path and am always working towards success in every field of being.

45. I love waking up with positive energy and vigor every day.

46. I am a source of inspiration to both myself and others.

47. I walk a path of light and love and show others how to do the same.

48. I am strong enough to achieve all my goals

49. No thank you I would not like a cigarette, I would not like a cigarette, I would not like a cigarette,

50. I would like to sit in the non smoking section please

51. I would like a non smoking room please

52. No thanks, I don't smoke

53. Smoking is not something I'm accustomed to, I don't like the taste of cigarettes
54. It's cold outside, I don't want to leave the room to smoke
55. Anything is possible for me in this day and age
56. My new body is healthier than I ever was before, and I will treat my body like it is worth something
57. I am not irritable at all today
58. The most important person in my life is me, because when I am happy, I will be able to make others happy
59. I love waking up in the morning and spending the day working towards my goals
60. I can do anything I set my mind to with great satisfaction and drive
61. I love everything about my life, including the people in it – I am blessed to be alive today
62. I cannot control the past, but I can control the present, and by doing that, I will control the future
63. Anything is possible if I just believe in myself
64. Success comes easy to me, because I have the Law of Attraction on my side, so I can magnetize the things I want to occur in life
65. I am moving towards my goals every single day
66. I keep getting better and better with each hour that passes by
67. I love who I am, and I love what I do
68. I leave each day a better person than I started it.

69. I am kind and happy, people love being around me and show that I can seek knowledge.
70. I am a wonderful spirit and walk the path of greatness every single day.

Now, it's time to return to your conscious mind.

Begin by slowly wiggling your toes, as you begin to return to the surface level.

You can feel yourself rising up back up into the conscious world.

You'll begin to feel sensation in your fingers...

At the top of your head.

And up from the base of your spine, to the top of your head.

Now, I will begin counting upwards, with each number, you will elevate your consciousness a little more.

When I reach five, you can open your eyes.

You will feel healed, loved, and warm inside.

You will feel positively energized throughout your body.

One. Moving slowly towards your conscious state.

Two. Your arms and legs will now have more weight on them.

Three. Pay attention to the room you are in, and feel the air around you.

Four. Your eyes are ready now.

Five. Open your eyes now, you can begin to stretch and enjoy what you just experienced.

Powerful Self Affirmations to Quit Drinking

Do not listen to this audio recording while driving or operating heavy machinery. Thank you.

Welcome to this guided meditation for allowing the Law of Attraction to help you quit drinking, look better, feel healthier and get the best out of your life.

It is recommended you listen to this recording for 21 days straight to unlock the true power of the Law of Attraction principles.

Now, if you haven't used a guided meditation or hypnosis tape before, it's important to know that you understand what is happening to your body throughout this recording.

When you are in the state of self hypnosis, you are not asleep, nor are you unconscious.

You're actually very aware of your surroundings, and you can't be coerced into doing anything which you don't want to.

So don't worry about any external distractions or noises because you will soon be able to relax completely.

You are always in complete control of yourself.

I will be saying a series of prompts, you can hear the suggestions and prompts as you wish.

Just allow yourself to absorb the suggestions without thinking or trying to analyze them.

And don't worry if your mind drifts off somewhere else.

You will still gain a positive outcome from the prompts and if you find yourself focusing on other thoughts, you can slowly remind yourself to focus only on my voice and what I am saying.

And don't worry if you don't think you are "getting it" or doing it right. Especially if this is your first time. There is no right or wrong way to go about this.

Just allow yourself to feel comfortable and relaxed.

And begin by taking a few deep breaths.

Breathe in through your nose, and out through your mouth.

And if you want, count the breathes as they come.

So if your mind wanders, just bring your focus back the breath.

Just breath in through your nose, and out through your mouth.

Now, I will begin the affirmations which will assist you on your journey to quit drinking.

1. I do not require alcohol to be a functioning member of society

2. I am a continued positive presence in my life and the lives of others.

3. Everything is possible for I am of sound mind and pure heart.

4. With the Law of Attraction on my side, I can do anything I set my mind to

5. Nothing is impossible for me, because I know what is best for myself – and what is best for me as a person

6. I surround myself with a strong, positive support system who help reinforce my higher goals here on this Earth

7. I love waking up every morning and seeing the progress I have made in my journey

8. I do not need to drink today

9. I can conquer any challenge in front of me, simply by using my willpower

10. The universe is on my side and helps me with reaching my goals

11. My will is unstoppable and I can achieve anything that I set my mind to

12. I keep moving towards my goals with full force of energy, because I know I am strong enough to achieve anything

13. I am a good person, and my past actions do not reflect on who I am today

14. I cannot change the past, but I can change the present, and by doing that I can change my future

15. With the power of self hypnosis, anything is possible, and I am using this on my journey to quit drinking, one day at a time

16. I may have hurt people in my past, but I will make sure that I don't hurt anyone in the future

17. My life right now is wonderful and it will continue to be even better every day that I am on this Earth.

18. I approach each day with a positive mental attitude.

19. I am a kind and wonderful person and know how to best leverage my skills for maximum success.

20. I am a great asset to society, and the world is a better place with me on the planet

21. I love who I am, and I love the person I am becoming on this journey

22. I embrace every day and the challenges it brings, because I know this will make me stronger

23. I am a stronger person today than I was yesterday, and by knowing this – I can achieve anything I set my mind to

24. I continue to have a strong support system around me, and a network of people who understand my goals and will do everything in their power to help me get to where I want to be

25. I am a source of inspiration to both myself and others.

26. I walk a path of light and love and show others how to do the same.

27. It is truly easy to be a sober person

28. No thank you, I don't drink

29. I don't drink because I don't want to drink

30. I'll have a club soda please

31. I'll have a diet coke please

32. I did not drink today

33. I can walk into any environment and know that I am a strong person who can withstand any obstacle that life throws at me

34. I am happy and healthy today and I will be happier and healthier tomorrow

35. Life is great, and I can do anything that I set my mind to

36. I will always move towards my higher purpose on this earth, even if that particular path is more difficult in the short term

37. I have been alcohol free for 7 days now

38. I work towards my goals every day, and understand that I have a long term view of things

39. I do not drink alcohol

40. My past decisions do not reflect who I am as a person today

41. The Law of Attraction is on my side and I can magnetize anything I want, and I choose to magnetize health and wellness in my life

42. I am walking on a path of longevity

43. I can breathe freely with grace and ease

44. I go to bed at night knowing that I gave the day my best effort
45. I am a path to freedom from alcohol
46. I have been alcohol free for 30 days now
47. Nothing can stop me from reaching my ultimate goals
48. Any challenge in front of me is something I'm going to embrace because I know that life is full of challenges, but I am strong enough to endure them
49. I am thankful for my friends and family for supporting me in my goals
50. I have been alcohol free for 1 year now
51. I wish not for an easy life, but for the strength to endure a difficult one
52. I am a calm and patient person
53. A health life is the life for me
54. I can control my own destiny, and I understand what it takes to be great on this Earth
55. I can overcome any challenge, because I have the strengthen to do so
56. I have been alcohol free for 10 years now
57. I move towards my goals with ferocious speed and energy
58. No thank you, I don't drink
59. I don't drink because I don't want to drink
60. I'll have a club soda please
61. I'll have a diet coke please
62. I did not drink today

63. I am not irritable at all today

64. I have no cravings today

65. I attract the best possible people into my life.

66. I continue to amaze myself at the progress I have made recently.

67. Everyone is commenting about how good I like, and I feel good as well

68. I can truly see myself as the person I always wanted to be

69. I understand how to use the Law of Attraction to give me anything which I desire in life.

70. My life right now is wonderful and it will continue to be even better every day that I am on this Earth.

71. I do not drink alcohol

Now, it's time to return to your conscious mind.

Begin by slowly wiggling your toes, as you begin to return to the surface level.

You can feel yourself rising up back up into the conscious world.

You'll begin to feel sensation in your fingers...

At the top of your head.

And up from the base of your spine, to the top of your head.

Now, I will begin counting upwards, with each number, you will elevate your consciousness a little more.

When I reach five, you can open your eyes.

You will feel healed, loved, and warm inside.

You will feel positively energized throughout your body.

One. Moving slowly towards your conscious state.

Two. Your arms and legs will now have more weight on them.

Three. Pay attention to the room you are in, and feel the air around you.

Four. Your eyes are ready now.

Five. Open your eyes now, you can begin to stretch and enjoy what you just experienced.

Powerful Self Affirmations to Stop Procrastinating

Do not listen to this audio recording while driving or operating heavy machinery. Thank you.

Welcome to this guided meditation for allowing the law of attraction to help you stop procrastinating, get much done, master productivity and get the best out of your life.

It is recommended you listen to this recording for 21 days straight to unlock the true power of the Law of Attraction principles.

Now, if you haven't used a guided meditation or hypnosis tape before, it's important to know that you understand what is happening to your body throughout this recording.

When you are in the state of self hypnosis, you are not asleep, nor are you unconscious.

You're actually very aware of your surroundings, and you can't be coerced into doing anything which you don't want to.

So don't worry about any external distractions or noises because you will soon be able to relax completely.

You are always in complete control of yourself.

I will be saying a series of prompts, you can hear the suggestions and prompts as you wish.

Just allow yourself to absorb the suggestions without thinking or trying to analyze them.

And don't worry if your mind drifts off somewhere else.

You will still gain a positive outcome from the prompts and if you find yourself focusing on other thoughts, you can slowly remind yourself to focus only on my voice and what I am saying.

And don't worry if you don't think you are "getting it" or doing it right. Especially if this is your first time. There is no right or wrong way to go about this.

Just allow yourself to feel comfortable and relaxed.

And begin by taking a few deep breaths.

Breathe in through your nose, and out through your mouth.

And if you want, count the breathes as they come.

So if your mind wanders, just bring your focus back the breath.

Just breath in through your nose, and out through your mouth.

Now, I will begin the affirmations which will assist you on your journey to stop procrastinating.

1. I will conquer this day
2. I can do anything that is within my power

3. The universe is on my side, and with the powerful Law of Attraction, I can get anything done

4. I can overcome any challenge in my life, because I have the strength and energy to do so

5. My willpower is unstoppable, I have the force of 1000 suns

6. Nothing will stop me from reaching my highest goals

7. I surround myself with people who support and fulfill me. Their presence in my life will help me reach my goals

8. I love what I do, I will continue to love it for as long as I am doing it

9. Waking up in the morning is a blessing because I know exactly what I want to accomplish each day

10. Today will be a great day

11. My past decisions do not affect who I am today

12. I magnetize money into my life, money comes so easily to me

13. I can see my bank account growing each month

14. I am someone who finishes projects, I finish what I start

15. My goals are my main focus at the start of every day

16. I can't control the past, but I can control the present, and by controlling the present I will control my future

17. Greatness is coming to me and I can feel myself getting closer every single day

18. I know exactly what it takes to succeed and I am going out to execute on that vision

19. I can already see myself as having reached my goals, so I know the exact steps I need to take to get there

20. My family and friends love me, and I love them

21. I give back as much as I get

22. I do not have any distraction in life, for I am stronger than any pull which is lower than myself

23. Any step, no matter how small, is an important step towards my highest calling

24. Nothing is impossible for me, because I have the Law of Attraction on my side.

25. I know what it is that I want in life, and I know that I can achieve anything

26. There will be hurdles and challenges along the way, but I will not avoid them, I will embrace them because by conquering challenges, I make myself a stronger person going forward

27. It is important that I understand my limitations as a person, and work my life around them rather than trying to be somebody else

28. I am my own best friend and biggest asset in life's journey

29. I learn from the mistakes I have made in the past, so I will not make them in the future

30. I choose to surround myself with positive influences, and repel the negative people from my life

31. My path to greatness may not be straight, but it is the best path for me
32. I love who I am and I love what I do
33. Every single day is a learning opportunity for me
34. I am so excited to see what life has in store for me tomorrow
35. I can do anything
36. I set up my working environment to be distraction free
37. I will not have my head turned by lower frequencies
38. I can feel the ground beneath the soles of my feet
39. Nothing is impossible for me because I know exactly what it is I need to do in order to succeed
40. I love everything about my life
41. I can conquer any challenge and overcome any obstacle
42. I am moving towards my goals at a more rapid pace than I ever have before
43. I constantly keep growing as a person, and I am so excited to see who I will become in one day, one week, one month and one year from now
44. My dream life is coming closer and closer to me every day that I am alive.
45. I defy anyone who does not believe in my potential as a human being
46. I can create miracles on a daily basis.
47. Everybody who is worth knowing, is someone who will lift me up even when my spirits are waning

48. I attract positive people into my life and repel negative ones

49. There is an abundance of wealth and resources in the world, and I will have my fair share of them.

50. There is not a challenge on this Earth that is too difficult for me to overcome

51. I love the people close to me and I will provide them with everything they need to succeed.

52. Anything is possible if I just set my mind to it.

53. Each task I undertake today will move me closer to my ultimate lifestyle.

54. I have all the abilities to create financial freedom with myself and my loved ones.

55. I am a positive presence and I light up any room that I am in

56. I love who I am and I love who I am becoming

57. Every new day on this Earth is an opportunity for me to learn and to grow as a human

58. I am pure light and love, I am pure spirit and the Universe will reward me for giving this good energy, by giving an equal amount of good energy back to me

59. I keep moving forward and I keep accomplishing my goals

60. I love the sheer potential of the human race

61. I am a creative problem solver who always knows who to overcome any challenges and conquer any obstacle in my way.

62. Every single obstacle is a learning experience for me

63. I am a joyous and wonderful being.

64. I surround myself with people who want me to accomplish my goals, and whose goals I want them to accomplish

65. My path to happiness is straightforward because I know what it is that I truly want and value in life.

66. Life is so great and I am truly blessed to be alive today

Now, it's time to return to your conscious mind.

Begin by slowly wiggling your toes, as you begin to return to the surface level.

You can feel yourself rising up back up into the conscious world.

You'll begin to feel sensation in your fingers...

At the top of your head.

And up from the base of your spine, to the top of your head.

Now, I will begin counting upwards, with each number, you will elevate your consciousness a little more.

When I reach five, you can open your eyes.

You will feel healed, loved, and warm inside.

You will feel positively energized throughout your body.

One. Moving slowly towards your conscious state.

Two. Your arms and legs will now have more weight on them.

Three. Pay attention to the room you are in, and feel the air around you.

Four. Your eyes are ready now.

Five. Open your eyes now, you can begin to stretch and enjoy what you just experienced.

Powerful Self Affirmations for Magnetizing Wealth

Do not listen to this audio recording while driving or operating heavy machinery. Thank you.

Welcome to this guided meditation for allowing the law of attraction to help you master your own destiny, magnetize money, manifest wealth and get the best out of your life.

It is recommended you listen to this recording for 21 days straight to unlock the true power of the Law of Attraction principles.

Now, if you haven't used a guided meditation or hypnosis tape before, it's important to know that you understand what is happening to your body throughout this recording.

When you are in the state of self hypnosis, you are not asleep, nor are you unconscious.

You're actually very aware of your surroundings, and you can't be coerced into doing anything which you don't want to.

So don't worry about any external distractions or noises because you will soon be able to relax completely.

You are always in complete control of yourself.

I will be saying a series of prompts, you can hear the suggestions and prompts as you wish.

Just allow yourself to absorb the suggestions without thinking or trying to analyze them.

And don't worry if your mind drifts off somewhere else.

You will still gain a positive outcome from the prompts and if you find yourself focusing on other thoughts, you can slowly remind yourself to focus only on my voice and what I am saying.

And don't worry if you don't think you are "getting it" or doing it right. Especially if this is your first time. There is no right or wrong way to go about this.

Just allow yourself to feel comfortable and relaxed.

And begin by taking a few deep breaths.

Breathe in through your nose, and out through your mouth.

And if you want, count the breathes as they come.

So if your mind wanders, just bring your focus back the breath.

Just breath in through your nose, and out through your mouth.

Now, I will begin the affirmations which will assist you on your journey to a happier, more fruitful life.

1. I can easily attract everything I want into my life

2. I know what it is I need to do in order to make a success of myself

3. Nothing will stop me from achieving my goals

4. I can overcome any challenge, obstacle or hurdle which may be in front of me

5. I embrace the struggles of daily life, because I know that this is what makes me stronger

6. I keep building on myself every single day and I continue to get better and better throughout life

7. I am not my past and my past is not me

8. I easily attract wealth and magnetize money towards me

9. I love to embrace new challenges throughout life

10. Any setback I have is merely temporary on my path to greatness

11. Even the smallest step is the start on an epic journey, and even the smallest progress towards my goals is worth it

12. Every day I wake up and I am proud of who I see in the mirror

13. I can and will achieve all of my goals, whether they be in the sphere of wealth, health or happiness

14. Movement over meditation

15. Everything is possible for me and I can move forward swiftly and firmly as a human being.

16. I am at one with the universe and I know full well that I can achieve anything I want in this life.

17. I am always striving to be the best version of myself and understand that happiness is my true calling and that financial freedom is coming to me sooner than I could have possibly imagined.
18. I am unlimited power in its purest form.
19. I surround myself with good and positive people, who support me in the pursuit of my goals. In turn I do the same for them.
20. I receive as much as I give from this world
21. I love everything about myself
22. Everything is possible for me to do for I am a superb human being and I know that I can do anything that I set my mind to.
23. If people do not support me or align with my goals, I remove them from my life
24. I am a wonderful person who is ready to receive all the gifts the universe has in store for me.
25. I cannot control the past, but I can control the present, and by controlling the present I can control my future
26. Not everyone shares my goals and dreams, but that is ok
27. I love my family and friends because they help me to reach my goals
28. My energy is aligned with the universe and money is flooding towards me at an alarming rate.
29. Money comes easily to me, because I know how to provide value to people in whatever form they desire it

30. My bank account is growing every single day I am alive.

31. I wake up every day with a smile on my face and a spring in my step

32. One die I will no longer be on this earth, so any trivial problem I may have is not worth thinking about

33. I always strive for greatness in everything I do.

34. I am feeling more and more assured of my success every single day that I am on this planet, for I am aligned with the universe and its wishes for me.

35. I continue to impress myself with the progress I have made

36. I am self-reliant, creative and always looking forward to creating more value for those around me at all times.

37. I love who I am, and I love the person I am becoming in this journey through life

38. I only choose to engage in high vibration activities

39. People can sense that I am operating in the zone

40. I know that I cannot be all things to all people, and I am at peace with that

41. I am moving in the right direction in life

42. I am a kind person who sends love out to others in whatever form they need it

43. I keep working in order to be the person I need to be to reach my highest calling

44. I understand that the more value I create for the world, the more money I will receive in return. And that this truth is universal.

45. Money is flowing towards me at a rapid rate, I am creating rivers of revenue in my life

46. I can get my dream job if I want to

47. I can attract my dream client if I want to

48. I can win the big account if I want to

49. I embrace the journey, not just the destination

50. I measure myself not by my material accomplishments, but by my character and the people I choose to surround myself with

51. I am a wonderful human being who is loved by the universe and everyone around me.

52. I am surrounding myself with good influences who will push me to greater things and understand that I am on this great path the universe has created for me.

53. I know what it is I have to do each day in order to improve

54. I know that stressful situations are only temporary on my path to greatness

55. I can achieve anything I desire and anything I set my mind to

56. I become what I think about, which is why I only think about success and happiness

57. I am operating on a higher plane of consciousness

58. I love surrounding myself with positive and supportive people

59. I can achieve everything I want in this life because I am aligned with the wishes of the universe and am I a creator of maximum wealth.

60. I choose to learn from people wiser than me

61. I spend my time engaged in productive and fruitful activities which will benefit me in innumerable ways

62. I am moving towards my goals at lightspeed because I know I am can achieve anything and everything I set my mind to.

63. I have a long term, delayed gratification mindset

64. I am love

65. I am light

66. I am spirit

67. I am hope

68. I am embracing the powerful Law of Attraction and know full well that this law will assist me on my path to greatness in all forms

Now, it's time to return to your conscious mind.

Begin by slowly wiggling your toes, as you begin to return to the surface level.

You can feel yourself rising up back up into the conscious world.

You'll begin to feel sensation in your fingers...

At the top of your head.

And up from the base of your spine, to the top of your head.

Now, I will begin counting upwards, with each number, you will elevate your consciousness a little more.

When I reach five, you can open your eyes.

You will feel healed, loved, and warm inside.

You will feel positively energized throughout your body.

One. Moving slowly towards your conscious state.

Two. Your arms and legs will now have more weight on them.

Three. Pay attention to the room you are in, and feel the air around you.

Four. Your eyes are ready now.

Five. Open your eyes now, you can begin to stretch and enjoy what you just experienced.

Made in the USA
Las Vegas, NV
13 April 2023

70540646R00090